DATE DUE			

THE MONTHLY CATALOG OF UNITED STATES GOVERNMENT PUBLICATIONS

AN INTRODUCTION TO ITS USE

JOHN GORDON BURKE AND CAROL DUGAN WILSON

LINNET BOOKS 1973

Library of Congress Cataloging in Publication Data

Burke, John Gordon, 1938–
    The monthly catalog of United States Government
publications.

    Bibliography: p.
    1. United States, Superintendent of Documents. Monthly
catalog of United States Government publications. I. Wilson,
Carol Dugan, 1947–   joint author. II. Title.
Z1223.A184   015'.73   72–11690

ISBN 0–208–01287–7

Contents

Introduction

This book is an introduction to the *Monthly Catalog of U.S. Government Publications*. It is intended to provide you with the skills necessary to use this reference tool, and to bibliographically identify the government document for which you have a reference or a citation. Chapter I provides a basic outline of the bibliographical elements essential to locating a government document. Chapter II provides the user of the *Monthly Catalog* with a few facts about the pattern of indexing in the *Monthly Catalog* and some of its features in order to facilitate its regular use. Since there are many government documents which do not make their way into the *Monthly Catalog*, Chapter III is devoted to a brief look at some of the additional sources to which a person may turn in order to locate an elusive government document. Chapter IV provides a listing of bibliographical aids to supplement the *Monthly Catalog* in locating an historical government document, and a bibliography of supplementary readings and the appendices provide additional listings of materials for the interested person.

It is hoped that this introductory manual will be of aid to persons using the *Monthly Catalog of U.S. Government Publications*. Government documents are both unique and useful sources of information for the researcher as well as for the general citizen. The *Monthly Catalog of U.S. Government Publications* has expanded its listing of documents in the past decade, yet without question the publication of government documents has expanded at an even greater rate. The *Monthly Catalog*, nonetheless, remains the major bibliographical tool for the control of government publications and the most important point of access to publications of our government. The researcher in social science and in science and industry must keep abreast of a number of documents regularly listed in the *Monthly Catalog*, and it is hoped that this handbook will provide the researcher as well as the layman with an elementary knowledge of the skills necessary to do so.

To librarians, our purpose in writing this book is to provide the unsophisticated library patron with the elementary skills necessary to use the *Monthly Catalog*, and thus save you, the librarian, the necessity of explaining these skills to the library patron, or as is more often the case, the necessity of actually exercising these skills for the patron to locate a document. This book is not intended to be a handbook to the *Monthly Catalog* for the professional librarian, though a handbook to the *Monthly Catalog* is needed and would be an invaluable reference book for the general reference librarian as well as most beginning document librarians.

The authors anticipate that there will be future revisions of this book, and as a result, request that criticisms or comments be directed to the authors in care of the publisher. It is our concern to provide a clear and useful guide to the *Monthly Catalog* for the general library patron, and your suggestions and recommendations about improving this book will be welcomed and very much appreciated.

I

The Essential Bibliographical Elements

Government documents are unique sources of information, but often elude the library user because they are difficult to locate bibliographically. The key to the successful use of government documents in library research is a thorough understanding of the use of the *Monthly Catalog of U.S. Government Publications,* and in this chapter we will present a step by step explanation of how to use this reference tool. For our purposes we will assume you are concerned with locating a specific government document on the sample pages of the *Monthly Catalog* which are reproduced, and indicate to you how you can have access to it through the *Monthly Catalog.*

The first step in locating a government document is the use of the index which appears in each issue, or the cumulative annual index which appears in the December issue of the *Monthly Catalog.* The cumulative index appearing in the December issue indexes the material contained in the *Monthly Catalog* from January to December. When using the index, you should be able to find the document you need by looking under one or more of four indexing categories: (1) subject heading, (2) author,[1] (3) unique title of a document, or (4) the government agency which published the document. Each document will have an index listing under two or perhaps three of these categories, but seldom under all four. You should remember when looking for a document by subject that subject listings can be further divided into specific as well as general subject headings. Now notice the number following the title (3) in the index (see fig. 1): this is the "entry number" and designates the order in which the document appears chronologically in the *Monthly Catalog* in a calendar year. It is important to keep in mind the index of the *Monthly Catalog* refers to documents in the body of the catalog by entry number, and when you have this number, you can find the actual entry containing the information about the document you are seeking. A common mistake that is made by users of the *Monthly Catalog* is to assume that numbers appearing in the index refer to page numbers. The entry number as an indexing device was first introduced in the *Monthly Catalog* in September 1947, and it is only before this date that the index refers to page numbers. Numbers appearing in the index of the *Monthly Catalog* currently refer to "entry numbers."

There are several essential bibliographical elements in each document entry, and two elements are absolutely essential to locating a document if it is to be used in microform. The first of these elements is the year of the *Monthly Catalog* in which the document appears. The second is the document entry number which was obtained from the index and which allows you to locate the document entry within the *Monthly Catalog*. In the document entry, this number appears at the beginning and to the left of the document title as you can see in figure 2. These two bibliographical elements are the only two bibliographical elements needed to locate and use a government document on microform.

Additional bibliographical elements are essential to identify and locate a document if it is to be used in its original form. The third bibliographical element is the government agency which published the document. Every government document is published by some government agency and in the *Monthly Catalog*, document entries are grouped together under issuing agencies. Further, these government agencies, with their subsequent document entries, appear alphabetically so that documents published by the Agriculture Department will appear before documents published by the Treasury Department in individual issues of the *Monthly Catalog*. A fourth essential element, the document's title, begins each entry, and the publication date of the document, the fifth element, appears only after the title, content notes which the catalog's editors find necessary, and the name of the individual author, if any. A sixth bibliographical element in a document entry is the depository notation and it is essential in establishing the availability of a government document.[2] If a solid black dot appears in the entry, this particular document has been sent to an official depository library and is available for your use. A complete list of depository libraries appears in Appendix VI. If the document entry does not contain a depository notation, then you must either use the document on microform, order the document for personal use, or borrow the document on interlibrary loan if it is not in your library. It is only in the first instance, viz. the use of the document on microform, that a library user has automatic access to the document even if the document is not a depository item. As a general rule of thumb, though, one must allow about six months before a document is available on microform after it appears in an issue of the *Monthly Catalog*.

A final bibliographical element essential to the physical location of a document is the Superintendent of Documents classification number. This classification number appears as the last item in a document entry, and in most cases is a very long number. Table I provides a listing of the essential bibliographical elements to (1) use a document on microform, (2) locate or ask a librarian for a document in its original form, and (3) order a personal copy of a government document.[3]

The important bibliographical elements of a document entry depend upon the form in which you intend to use the document. Many libraries carry the Readex microform edition of depository and nondepository U.S. Government publications. You must know the year of the *Monthly Catalog* in which the document is listed and the document's entry number to use the document in this form.[4] If you need to use the document in its original form, the most important element is the depository symbol indicating that this document has been sent to all depository libraries. In order for you or the librarian to find the document, you will need the following bibliographical information to locate the document: issuing government agency, title, date of publication, and Superintendent of Documents classification number. Unfortunately, documents which do not carry the depository symbol are usually only available from a regional documents depository and will have to be borrowed on interlibrary loan through your library.

If your original intent was to order your own copy of a government document, then you will need ordering information. The symbols used in the *Monthly Catalog* and explained inside the catalog's front cover will tell you where you may write for the document. In addition, you must supply the following information when ordering a document: issuing government agency, title, date of publication, price, special

TABLE I

NECESSARY BIBLIOGRAPHICAL ELEMENTS FOR USE OF
GOVERNMENT DOCUMENTS

Microform	Original Copy from Library	Original Copy for Purchase
1. Year of *Monthly Catalog* in which document appears	3. Issuing agency	8. Issuing agency
	4. Title	9. Title
2. Entry number	5. Date of Publication	10. Date of Publication
	6. Presence or absence of depository notation symbol	11. Price
		12. Series or stock number (if any)
	7. Superintendent of Documents classification number	13. Superintendent of documents classification number

agency ordering information if indicated (series or stock number), and Superintendent of Documents classification number. (See fig. 3.) Payment for documents must accompany the order and must always be made by GPO coupons, postal money order, express order or check. You may send currency, but it will be at your own risk. Deposit accounts can be opened for persons or institutions making frequent purchases of government documents, and special order blanks are supplied after a deposit account has been established. If you are not in the United States when ordering, foreign remittances can be made by using international money order or by using a draft on an American bank.

Finally, in some cases you will not be able to find a document you are seeking in the *Monthly Catalog*. This may occur with a recently published document not yet entered in the *Monthly Catalog*. In these instances, one must wait until the following month and see if the document appears then. However, there are some government documents which never appear in the *Monthly Catalog* and must be found elsewhere. In Chapter III, this area is explored by subject matter and additional reference tools are cited where some of these documents that have not been included in the *Monthly Catalog* can be found.

1. Personal authors were not indexed in the *Monthly Catalog* between the years 1947 and 1962.

2. Documents appearing in the *Monthly Catalog* are of two types: "depository" documents sent to all government document depository libraries, and "nondepository" documents which are not

sent automatically to government document depository libraries. As a result of the Documents Expediting Project and other acquisition efforts, many depository libraries have more complete document collections than indicated by the depository notation symbols in the *Monthly Catalog*.

3. When documents are ordered from the Superintendent of Documents, the document classification number must always be included. Inside the front cover of the *Monthly Catalog* is a list of symbols indicating the different places a document is to be ordered. Most documents are available from the Superintendent of Documents, U.S. Government Printing Office, Washington, D.C. 20402 and are marked by an asterisk. Documents for sale by the National Technical Information Service, Springfield, VA 22151 and other issuing offices are marked by special symbols. Documents printed for official use and not available for general distribution are also marked by a special symbol. All documents which are offered for sale and listed in the *Monthly Catalog* are priced.

4. The Readex microform edition of U.S. Government depository publications only covers the years 1956 to the present. Nondepository publications are available on microform from 1953 to the present. Prior to these dates, one must rely on the original documents.

INDEX

Whitehead, Clay T., nomination, hearings, 4743
Whitney, John H., nomination, hearings, 4745
Wholesale trade, census of business, 1967, subject reports, 4278
Wichita County, Kans., community profile, 5038
Wick, Herbert L., spacing trial in Australian toon, 5185
Widows and widowers, see Pensions.
Wild life, see Wildlife.
Wilderness areas, designate, hearings, 4660
① Wildlife:
grassland restoration and wildlife, 5739
restoration project, funds, additional, hearing, 4748
see also Natural resources.
Wilkin County, Minn., community profile, 5039
William "Bill" Dannelly Reservoir, Alabama River, designate, law, 4456
William C. Cramer Federal Office Building, St. Petersburg, Fla., name, law, 4526
William G. Stone Navigation Lock, designate navigation lock on Sacramento deepwater ship channel, Calif., law, 4447
Williams, John J., tributes upon occasion of his retirement from Senate, 4678
Wilmoth, Roger C., neutralization of high ferric iron acid mine drainage, 5888
② Wilson, Louis F.:
pine root collar weevil, 5158
hazard zones, for red pine in lower Michigan, 5168
red-headed pine sawfly, 5157
Wilson County, Kans., community profile, 5040
Wilson's Creek Battlefield National Park, authorize additional funds, and change name, law, 4427
Wilson's Creek National Battlefield, designate, law, 4427
Wilton, Brussels, velvet and tapestry carpets and rugs, 5822
Wind tunnels, investigation of jet transport airplane configuration with external flow jet flap and inboard pod-mounted engines, 5524
Winona County, Minn., community profile, 5041
③ Winter activities in national park system, 5637
Wire, see Electric wire and wiring.
Wire mesh, see Wire netting.
Wire netting, strainer elements, Federal item identification guide, 4823
Wisconsin, southwestern, forest floor characteristics, 5166
Withholding tax, see Income tax.
Women:
discrimination against women in federally assisted programs and in employment in education, extend Equal pay act to prohibit, 4650
print additional copies, reports, 4617, 4704
dual careers, longitudinal study of labor market experience, 5398
④ Women's Army Corps:
begin as executive, 4240
educational opportunities, exciting jobs, 4241
Wood, S. O. jr.:
sand and gravel, 5463
stone, 5465
Wood:
machining abstracts, 1968 and 1969 literature, 5212
products used in single-family houses inspected by FHA, 4202
Wood pulp:
pulpwood—
prices in Southeast, trends, 5190

Wood pulp—Continued
production, north central region by county, 5215
Woods, see Forests and forestry.
Woodson County, Kans., community profile, 5042
Woodworking machinery, woodworking machines safeguarding, 5402
Wool, America's wool, 6-cent commemorative postage stamp (poster), 5837
Work, safe work guide, Department of Labor safety training programs, LS series, 5402
Workbook, training course for voluntary income tax assistors, 5333
Workers, see Labor.
Workmen's compensation, see Employers liability and workmen's compensation.
World, see specific subjects.
World agricultural situation, 5057
World trade, see Commerce.
Worley, David P., "let-it-grow" treatment for timber, is it economically worthwhile? 5198
Wrangell, Alaska, Wrangell-Petersburg Election District, community profile, 5043
Wrather, Jack, nomination, hearings, 4745
Wrenches, and components, hand, nonpowered, Federal item identification guide, change, 4828
Wright County, Minn., community profile, 5044
Writing, contest for hospitalized veterans, 5879
Wrotnowski, Arthur C., fabrication of felt-membrane composites, 5304
Wyandotte County, Kans., community profile, 5045

X
X-ray photography, see Radiography.
X-rays, see Radiography.

Y
Yakima Indians, trust property, inheritance, repeal restriction, law, 4500
Yates, J. E., study of panel flutter with exact method of Zeydel, 5490
Yawney, Harry W., sugar maple planting study in Vermont, 5203
Yeagley, J. Walter, nomination, hearing, 4754
Yee, Clifford H., nomination, hearing, 4758
Yellow Medicine County, Minn., community profile, 5046
Yeomen 3 & 2, Navy training manual, 5662
You think you have problems?, 5474
Youth:
American, 1970, characteristics, population, education, etc., 4325
America's best hope, juvenile delinquency prevention and control act, 5907
interstate compact on juveniles, adoption by District of Columbia, hearing, 4753
youth in turmoil, 5606
Youth Opportunity, President's Council on, see President's Council on Youth Opportunity.
Yugoslavia, cotton textiles, trade agreement, 5800
Yukon, Alaska, Yukon-Koyukuk Election District, community profile, 5017

Z
Zenoria, see Beetles.
Zeydel, E. F. E., exact method of Zeydel, study of panel flutter, 5490
Zinc, ores, census of mineral industries, 1967, industry statistics, 4287
Zoology, Smithsonian contributions to zoology, 5718–20
Zwieback, E. L., investigation of DC–8 nacelle modifications to reduce fan-compressor noise in airport communities, flight acoustical and performance evaluation, 5485

Explanatory key:
1. Subject heading
2. Author
3. Title
4. Government Agency

Fig. 1   SAMPLE INDEX PAGE OF THE MONTHLY CATALOG

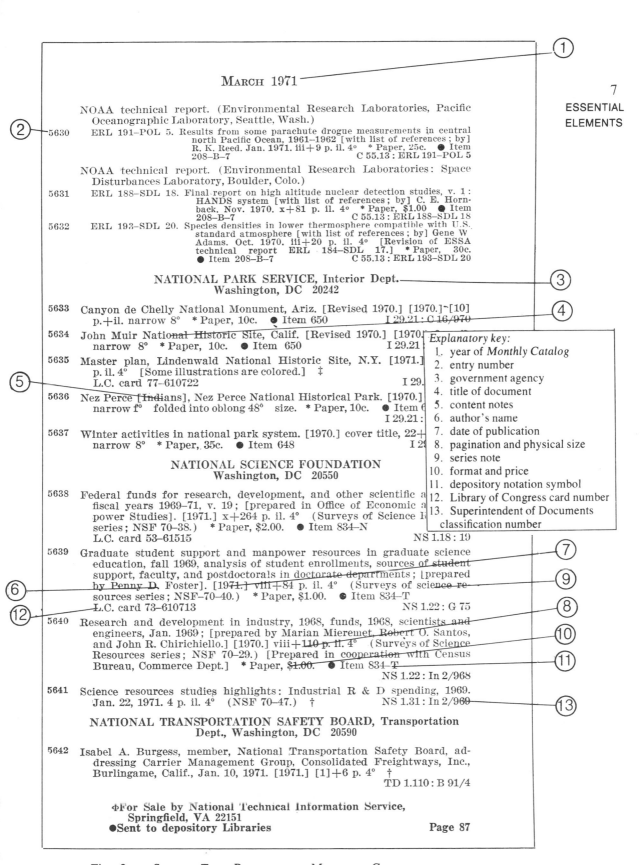

Fig. 2   SAMPLE TEXT PAGE OF THE MONTHLY CATALOG

Order Blank

To Superintendent of Documents,
Government Printing Office,
Washington, D.C.   20402

Date _____, 19____

Your name _____

Street address _____

City, State, and ZIP Code _____

Catalog number is shown at right-hand end of last line of entry in
Monthly Catalog.   Order *only* publications indicated by a star (*)
preceding the list price.

For Use of Supt. of Docs.

_____	Enclosed _____
_____	To be mailed later _____
_____	Subscriptions _____
	Refund_____
	Coupon refund _____
	Postage _____

CATALOG No.	QUANTITY DESIRED	TITLE OF PUBLICATION	AMOUNT

For additional space use other side.

Total, $ _____

For PROMPT, ACCURATE SHIPMENT please fill in the following label—Please PRINT or typewrite.

U.S. GOVERNMENT PRINTING OFFICE
PUBLIC DOCUMENTS DEPARTMENT
WASHINGTON, D.C.   20402

OFFICIAL BUSINESS

RETURN AFTER FIVE DAYS

POSTAGE AND FEES PAID
U.S. GOVERNMENT PRINTING OFFICE

Name _____

Street Address _____

City, State, and ZIP Code _____

Fig. 3

It is essential to include the Superintendent of Documents Classification Number or the "Catalog" number when ordering publications from the Superintendent of Documents. Only those items marked by an asterisk or star (*) preceding the list price are available from the Government Printing Office. Institutions or individuals ordering from abroad may remit either by international money order or draft on an American bank. Foreign remittances generally must cover the cost of postage. In computing foreign postage, add one-fourth of the price of the publication.

II

Indexing and Features of the
Monthly Catalog

Each issue of the *Monthly Catalog of U.S. Government Publications* is accompanied by an index. Bibliographical information on specific documents will be found within the *Monthly Catalog*, and it is in the cumulative annual index that one must first seek his document unless one has an author citation, in which case a short cut is possible through the use of a personal author index to the *Monthly Catalog*. The indexing which characterizes the *Monthly Catalog* has evolved over the history of this reference tool, and four sample pages reproduced here indicate some of the more obvious patterns of development.

For users of a government document that is a minimum of two years old, it is undoubtedly easier to locate and use the document in microform, provided the document was published after 1956 or 1953 if it is a nondepository government document. For documents listed in the *Monthly Catalog* prior to this date, one must use the document in the original, for these older government documents are not currently available on microform.

The *Monthly Catalog* and its predecessors were intended as a record of government publication for Congress as well as a reference tool designed to indicate the availability and location of government documents. Publications offered for sale by the Superintendent of Documents were first indicated in 1895. It was not until 1942, though, that the depository notation was first introduced as a device in the

SAMPLE INDEX PAGES OF THE MONTHLY CATALOG

The evolution of indexing in the *Monthly Catalog* is marked by increased use of subject subdivisions (cf. 1924–25); use of running heads for informational purposes (cf. 1934); and introduction of document "entry numbers" (cf. 1954).

SAMPLE INDEX PAGES OF THE MONTHLY CATALOG

Monthly Catalog. Consequently, it is only after this date that one can know from the *Monthly Catalog* if an institution is supposed to have a government document provided the library had depository status at the time of the document's publication. Because of the complexities of determining whether an individual institution received a government document carrying a depository notation, the depository notation is really only useful in determining if an institution has a current document. All depository libraries should have recent files of U.S. government documents carrying a depository notation, and patrons using the *Monthly Catalog* in a nondepository institution can reasonably expect to find a copy of these documents in depository libraries. For the person in search of an older document, the depository notation is less useful, though it does indicate the document should be in a depository library provided the library had depository status at the time of the document's publication.

The Government Printing Office over the years has evolved a system of classification for government documents, and in 1924 this classification system was introduced in the *Monthly Catalog.* The complete schedule of the Superintendent of Document's classification scheme is contained in Appendix II. Documents appearing in the *Monthly Catalog* prior to 1924 were often catalogued by libraries in the Dewey Decimal classification system. After the introduction of the Superintendent of Documents classification scheme, however, most institutions maintaining documents collections adopted this scheme, and hence one must have the Superintendent of Document's classification number to find documents in these collections. For documents in library collections prior to the introduction of the Superintendent of Documents classification scheme, one must consult the library's general public catalog provided the documents have not been integrated into a general documents collection.

It was previously mentioned that a short cut to the use of the *Monthly Catalog* exists if one has a personal author citation to a government document. The Government Printing Office did issue a decennial personal author index for the years 1941 to 1950 and 1951 to 1960. These indexes can be found with every set of the *Monthly Catalog.* The Pieran Press, however, has carried on the early indexing work of the GPO, and has issued cumulative author indexes for the years 1941 to 1965. The *Cumulative Personal Author Index for the Monthly Catalog of United States Publications* provides a handy shortcut to the use of the *Monthly Catalog* annual indexes if one has a citation to the document by personal author.

A distinctive feature which can in addition come to the aid of the *Monthly Catalog* user is the annual list of U.S. government serials which appears each year in the February issue. The list of serials first appeared in 1962, and has appeared annually since that time. It should be noted, however, since a number of government serial publications are directed at both general and special audiences, libraries have felt little compulsion to keep these government serial publications in a centralized documents collection. Frequently, they are placed in other areas of the library by subject, and hence it is often the general public catalog in libraries which must be used to locate them.

For the *Monthly Catalog* user who is not seeking a specific document, but instead wishes to keep abreast of new government publications in selected subject areas issued by the Government Printing Office, the regular feature "previews" is a section of the *Monthly Catalog* which should be consulted. First begun in January, 1948, this service provides a monthly look ahead to documents which will be issued by the U.S. government.

The use of U.S. government publications is facilitated through the existence of depository libraries and before concluding this chapter, it would be helpful to note their history. Enacted in 1895, the General Printing Act provided for the regular deposit of a broad range of U.S. government publications in a number of institutions around the country. A list of the current depository institutions with date of the inception of depository status may be found in Appendix VI.[1] Currently, there are 1,036 selective depositories and 39 regional document depositories. Under current law, a selective depository can discard any document it wishes after first obtaining permission from the regional documents depository to do so. As a result, even though a document is a recent depository item, this does not mean the patron will find it in every depository institution, for it may well have been discarded or sent to the regional depository for its document collection. In this case, the document should be available on interlibrary loan, following regular interlibrary loan procedures. It should be remembered, however, that government documents are not copyright; hence, personal copies for the cost of photocopying are available to all individuals desiring them.

---

1. Appendix V (Designated Depository Libraries: History of Early Legislation) provides an explanation of why some institutions held depository status prior to 1895. Public Law 92-368, passed by the 92nd Congress, designates the highest state appellate court library as a depository of U.S. Government documents, and therefore a possible 46 additional libraries may be included in the depository library program.

III

Additional Sources for Government Documents

The rapid increase in the rate of publication of government documents in recent years as well as increased support on the part of the federal government for scholarly research has lead to the publication of many documents of scientific and scholarly interest which often do not find their way into the *Monthly Catalog*. For the researcher these documents are often problematic to find and one must turn to other bibliographical tools in order to locate them. The logical place to find a document of this type often depends upon its subject matter and in an effort to aid the researcher in finding a document which he identifies as a government document but cannot locate in the *Monthly Catalog*, a listing of additional bibliographical tools which frequently carry these documents has been prepared.

Research and Development Reports. A great many documents of scientific interest will be found in the *Government Reports Index* (formerly the *U.S. Government Research and Development Reports Index*), Superintendent of Documents classification number (C51.9/3: v. nos. & nos.). This bibliographical catalog presents a listing of government R&D reports which can be purchased from the National Technical Information Service (NTIS), Springfield, VA. 22151, and catalogs thousands of government research and development reports each year. The user of the *Monthly Catalog* who is not able to find a government document and is convinced that the document is a research and development report will want to first turn to this tool as the logical place to locate a document after a search of the *Monthly Catalog* has proved unsuccessful. Government R&D reports can be ordered from the National Technical Information Service unless specified otherwise in the entry and details for ordering these reports may be found in individual issues of the index.

Another source for government research reports that often don't appear in the *Monthly Catalog* is the *Public Affairs Information Service*. This index, which is a selective index covering the broad spectrum of public affairs, indexes a number of government documents in the social sciences. Among these documents listed may be found contract reports financed by various government agencies which do not make their way into the *Monthly Catalog*. These reports, when they do appear, can be found under personal author or subject in the PAIS, and the index is an invaluable tool to the researcher in the social sciences.

Documentation in Science. There are a number of sources in which government documents of a scientific nature can be found. Two important indexes are the *Bibliography of Agriculture* and the *Index Medicus*. These indexes, compiled by the national libraries of agriculture and medicine, provide complete bibliographical documentation for the subject areas of agriculture and medicine. A number of government documents, as a result, are indexed in these bibliographical tools which do not appear in the *Monthly Catalog*. Users of the *Monthly Catalog* whose interests fall into these specialized areas will usually consult these indexes as a matter of course. But for the person with an occasional interest in agriculture or medicine, these indexes provide a back-up to the *Monthly Catalog's* indexing in these two areas, and should be consulted if the *Monthly Catalog* does not provide a bibliographical citation for the document that is being sought. A third bibliographical source for documents of a scientific nature is *Nuclear Science Abstracts*. This is, again, a bibliography which will be of use only to the specialized researcher, but it does provide comprehensive coverage in this area.

Documentation in Education. The field of education is one of the most thoroughly documented fields of research. This is due primarily to the documentation efforts of the monthly abstract journal *Research in Education*, published by the National Center for Educational Communication. *Research in Education* publishes abstracts prepared by the nineteen clearinghouses funded by the U.S. Office of Education to document research in education. ERIC clearinghouses, which also prepare bibliographies and interpretive summaries of research for

Research in Education, prepare abstracts on research in education on the following topics: adult education; counseling and personnel services; the disadvantaged; early childhood education; educational management; educational media and technology; exceptional children; higher education; junior colleges; languages and linguistics; library and information sciences; reading; rural education and small schools; science, mathematics, and environmental education; social studies/social science education; teacher education; teaching of English; tests, measurement, and evaluation; and vocational and technical education.

Most of the research which is abstracted in *Research in Education* does not appear in the *Monthly Catalog,* because it is for the most part research that is published through the regular channels of scholarly publishing. It is, nonetheless, research which often is represented as a government document because of ERIC's program of microfilming the original documents abstracted in the index. For this reason, if the *Monthly Catalog* does not immediately yield the document you are seeking, it is best to consult *Research in Education.*

Congressional Documentation. The documents of the U.S. Congress which are featured in the popular press often never make their way into the *Monthly Catalog.* In 1970, the Congressional Index Service began a comprehensive indexing program for the publications of Congress with the *CIS Index,* and it is an index that should be consulted if a government document is a publication of Congress, and cannot be located in the *Monthly Catalog.*

IV

Sources for Historical
Government Documents

The *Monthly Catalog of U.S. Government Publications* has been
published continuously since 1885. The preface in the first issue of the
Monthly Catalog stated "Examination of these pages will reveal an
unexpectedly large number of subjects which have a public interest
quite apart from mere legislation". It has been the object of the
Monthly Catalog to bring these documents to the attention of the
general public, and fortunately the public is now able to acquire
government documents at a 'nominal cost'. There are bibliographic
aids other than the *Monthly Catalog* for identifying and locating
historical government documents, however, and the library patron
doing research with this type of material will want to be aware of these
reference tools and their chronological scope.

1789-1817: Greely, Adolphus Washington. *Public Documents of the
First Fourteen Congresses, 1789-1817. Papers relating to Early
Congressional Documents.* Washington: Government Printing Office,
1900.

>   This publication, also Senate Document 428, 56th Congress, 1st
> session, provides a bibliographical listing for about 5,000
> publications. A supplement to Greely, reprinted from the *Annual
> Report* of the American Historical Association, 1903 (volume 1,
> pp. 343-406), was published by the Government Printing Office in

1904. It currently has been reprinted by the Johnson Reprint Corporation.

1774-1881: Poore, Benjamin Perley. *A Descriptive Catalogue of the Government Publications of the United States, September 5, 1774 - March 4, 1881.* Washington: Government Printing Office, 1885.

First issued as Senate miscellaneous document 67, 48th Congress, 2nd session, it has been reprinted by Johnson Reprint Corporation.

1881-1893: Ames, John Griffith. *Comprehensive Index to the Publications of the United States Government, 1881-1893.* Washington: Government Printing Office, 1905.

This two volume bibliography was first published as House document 754, 58th Congress, 2nd session. It has also been reprinted by Johnson Reprint Corporation and like its predecessors, emphasizes Congressional publications.

1789-1909: U.S. Superintendent of Documents. *Checklist of United States Public Documents, 1789-1909.* 3rd edition. Washington: Government Printing Office, 1911.

A bibliography of documents arranged by government agency. It has been reprinted by Kraus Reprint.

There is a remaining bibliographical tool which can be confused with the *Monthly Catalog.* It is the *Catalog of the Public Documents of Congress and of All Departments of the Government of the United States for period March 4, 1893 - December 31, 1940,* and is commonly known as the *Documents Catalog.* The *Documents Catalog* is published in twenty-five volumes and is a dictionary catalog of both Congressional and agency publications. Published biannually until 1945, it is often used in lieu of the *Monthly Catalog* to locate a document issued between 1893 and 1940.

The user of the *Monthly Catalog* may on occasion want to make use of the *Documents Catalog* in locating a particular document which has been issued. To locate a document which has been issued prior to 1893, one must of necessity turn to the historical bibliographies previously mentioned. There are, in addition, reprints of various department's library catalogs that have recently been published, and the specialized researcher may want and need to turn upon occasion to one of these catalogs, e.g., *Subject Catalog of the Department Library,* United States Department of Health, Education and Welfare. (G.K. Hall, 1965). It is nonetheless the *Monthly Catalog of U.S. Government Publications* which remains the staple bibliography of government publication, and it is within its pages that most government documents sought by the library patron can be found.

V

Bibliography

This brief annotated bibliography is designed to provide additional sources of information about government documents for the library patron. Materials have been selected to provide general information as well as self-help aids in locating a document.

Andriot, John L. *Guide to U.S. Government Serials & Periodicals.* McLean, Va.: Documents Index, 1969-.

> This guide provides complete bibliographical information on U.S. government serials. Information about frequency, cost, Superintendent of Document classification number and Library of Congress card number is provided. Extremely useful for the ephemeral or little known serial. Each item is indexed by title, subject, and agency.

Boyd, Anne Morris. *United States Government Publications.* 3rd edition revised by Rae Elizabeth Rips. New York: H.W. Wilson, 1949.

> Commonly known as Boyd and Rips, this general introduction to government publications was for many years the standard guide to government publications. It has sections on most branches of the federal government and the significant publications of each federal agency are listed. Now out of date, it is nonetheless an important tool in understanding the broad range of government document publication.

Leidy, William P. *A Popular Guide to Government Publications*. 3rd edition. New York: Columbia University Press, 1968.

> In this guide to general government publications, documents are listed under broad subject headings. Now in its third edition, it can be used as a short cut in identifying a widely known or generally useful government document. Approximately 3,000 publications are included in the third edition.

O'Hara, Frederic J. "Selected Government Publications." In *Wilson Library Bulletin*. Monthly except July and August. New York: H.W. Wilson.

> This regular column in the *Wilson Library Bulletin* provides the reader with a selective guide to new government publications. Occasionally, it supplies invaluable information about government publications on timely topics. It can be a useful source of information if it is regularly read.

Schmeckebier, Laurence F. and Roy B. Eastin. *Government Publications and Their Use*. Revised edition. Washington, D.C.: Brookings Institution, 1961.

> This is currently the most complete and up-to-date general introduction to government documents. For information about government publications and document distribution, this should be the student's first source of information.

Wisdom, Donald S. and William P. Kilroy. *Popular Names of U.S. Government Reports: A Catalog*. Washington, D.C.: Library of Congress (Serial Division, Reference Department), 1966.

> A guide to government documents which have become identified with a personal name. This index allows the user to locate a document by its official title. A particularly useful reference tool for older government reports. A new edition of this work has been prepared by Bernard A. Bernier, Jr., and Charlotte M. David in 1970. Superintendent of Documents classification number: LC 6.2: G74/970.

Wynkoop, Sally. *Government Reference Books 68/69*. Littleton, Colorado: Libraries Unlimited, Inc., 1970.

> A biennial guide to government reference books arranged under broad subject dategories with over 600 titles listed in the first edition. An excellent guide to recent reference works published by the U.S. Government Printing Office.

Appendix I

*Superintendent of Documents
Classification Scheme*

LIST OF CLASSES OF UNITED STATES GOVERNMENT PUBLICATIONS AVAILABLE FOR SELECTION BY DEPOSITORY LIBRARIES

Revised June 30, 1972

Public Documents Department, U.S. Government Printing Office, Washington, D.C. 20402

NOTE.—Numbers following series titles are depository item numbers. The notation "Non-GPO" before the item number indicates the publications are not printed through the facilities of the Government Printing Office and that depository copies for the series are supplied by the issuing agency.

AGRICULTURE DEPARTMENT

(Secretary's Office and Department Series)

A 1.1:	Annual Report 6
A 1.2:	General Publications 10
A 1.9:	Farmers' Bulletins 9
A 1.10:	Yearbook 17
A 1.11/3:	Handbooks, Manuals, Guides 11–C
A 1.34:	Statistical Bulletins 15
A 1.35:	Leaflets 12
A 1.36:	Technical Bulletins 16
A 1.38:	Miscellaneous Publications 13–A
A 1.47:	Agricultural Statistics 1
A 1.58/a:	Agriculture Decisions 2
A 1.68:	PA [Program Aid] Series 14–A
A 1.75:	Agric. Information Bulletins 4
A 1.76:	Agriculture Handbooks 3
A 1.77:	Home and Garden Bulletins 11
A 1.82:	Marketing Research Reports 13–B
A 1.84:	Production Research Reports 13–C
A 1.86:	Household Food Consumption Survey Reports 11–A
A 1.87:	Home Economics Research Reports 11–B
A 1.88:	Utilization Research Reports 16–A
A 1.89/3:	Directories 6–A
A 1.92:	National Fire Prevention Week 13–E
A 1.95:	Marketing Bulletins 13–G
A 1.96:	National Farm Safety Week 13–H
A 1.99:	Periodic Reports of Agric. Economics (annual) 13–I
A 1.104:	Science Study Aids 14–B

Forest Service

A 13.1:	Annual Report 80
A 13.2:	General Publications 84
A 13.10:	National Forest Areas 86
A 13.11/2:	Lists of Publications 85–A
A 13.13:	Information Pamphlets Relating to National Forests 85
A 13.31:	American Woods 80–A
A 13.32:	Fire Control Notes 82
A 13.36:	Regulations, Rules, & Instructions 86–B
A 13.36/2:	Handbooks, Manuals, Guides 86–C
A 13.50:	Forest Resource Reports 83
A 13.51:	Tree Planters' Notes 86–D
A 13.52:	Forest Pest Leaflets 82–A
A 13.52/2:	Forest Insect Conditions in U.S. (annual) 82–B
A 13.55:	Forest Service Films Available on Loan for Educational Purposes (annual) 83–A
A 13.72:	Conservation Teaching Aids 81–A
A 13.86:	Forest Service Comments on Resolutions Relating to the National Forest System as Adopted 82–C

National Agricultural Library

A 17.2:	General Publications 95
A 17.17:	Library Lists 95–A

Information Office

A 21.2:	General Publications 90
A 21.6/5:	Bimonthly List of Publications and Motion Pictures 92
A 21.9/8:	List of Available Publications and Congressional Lists 91
A 21.28:	Handbooks, Manuals, Guides 90–A

General Counsel

A 33.2:	General Publications 124
A 33.7:	Laws 125

Federal Extension Service

A 43.2:	General Publications 61
A 43.4:	Circulars (numbered) 59–A
A 43.7:	Extension Service Review 60
A 43.16:	Regulations, Rules, & Instructions 61–A
A 43.16/2:	Handbooks, Manuals, Guides 61–B

Personnel Office

A 49.2:	General Publications 97
A 49.8:	Handbooks, Manuals, Guides 97

Soil Conservation Service

A 57.1/2:	Conservation Highlights, Digest of Progress Report of Soil Conservation Service 119–B
A 57.2:	General Publications 120
A 57.6/2:	Handbooks, Manuals, Guides 120–A
A 57.9:	Soil Conservation (monthly) 122
A 57.38:	Soil Survey Reports 102 (Rev. 1957)
A 57.38:list/	List of Published Soil Surveys 102–A
A 57.44:	Conservation Information SCS-CI-Series 119–A
A 57.52:	Soil Survey Investigation Reports 121–A

Federal Crop Insurance Corporation

A 62.1:	Annual Report 70 (Rev. 1970)
A 62.2:	General Publications 71
A 62.6/2:	Regulations, Rules, & Instructions 72

Foreign Agricultural Service

A 67.2:	General Publications 77
A 67.7/2:	Foreign Agriculture, including Foreign Crops and Markets 76
A 67.16:	Foreign Agricultural Reports 76–E
A 67.26:	Miscellaneous Series (FAS–M–Nos.) 76–G
A 67.35:	U.S. Report to FAO (triennial) 76–H

Rural Electrification Administration

A 68.1:	Annual Report 115
A 68.1/2:	Annual Statistical Report, Rural Elec. Borrowers 115
A 68.1/3:	Annual Statistical Report, Rural Telephone Borrowers 115
A 68.2:	General Publications 116
A 68.3:	Bulletins 116
A 68.5:	Laws 116–B

A 68.6/2:	List of Materials Acceptable for Use on Systems of REA Electrification Borrowers 116–A
A 68.6/4:	Telephone Engineering and Construction Manual 116–A
A 68.6/5:	List of Materials Acceptable for Use on Telephone Systems of REA Borrowers 116–A
A 68.14:	Addresses 115–A

Agricultural Research Service

A 77.2:	General Publications 26
A 77.6/3:	Handbooks, Manuals, Guides 26–A
A 77.10:	Addresses 25–A–1
A 77.12:	Agricultural Research 25–A
A 77.15:	ARS Numbered Series 25–B
A 77.20:	General Catalogue of Homoptera 25–C
A 77.22:	USDA Consumer Expenditure Survey Reports 26–B
A 77.23:	Conservation Research Reports 25–D
A 77.202:	General Publications Relating to Care of Animals & Poultry 30
A 77.206:	Rules & Regulations Relating to Care of Animals & Poultry 32
A 77.206/2:	Handbooks, Manuals, Guides Relating to Care of Animals & Poultry 30–A
A 77.219:	Index-Catalogue of Medical and Veterinary Zoology 31
A 77.219/2:	——Supplements 31
A 77.219/3:	——by subject 31
A 77.219/4:	Index-Catalogue of Medical and Veterinary Zoology, Special Publications (numbered) 31
A 77.302:	General Publications Relating to Entomology & Plant Quarantine 44
A 77.306:	Regulations, Rules, & Instructions Relating to Entomology & Plant Quarantine 47
A 77.308:	Service & Regulatory Announcements Relating to Plant Pest Control 48
A 77.308/2:	List of Intercepted Plant Pests (annual) 48
A 77.308/5:	Plant Regulatory Announcements 48
A 77.320:	Picture Sheets 46
A 77.325:	Notices of Judgment under Federal Insecticide, Fungicide & Rodenticide Act 109
A 77.502:	General Publications Relating to Horticulture 100
A 77.511:	Plant Disease Reporter 100–B
A 77.515:	Plant Inventory 101
A 77.526:	National Arboretum Contribution 100–A
A 77.526/2:	National Arboretum Leaflets 100–A
A 77.602:	General Publications Relating to Dairy Research 42
A 77.702:	General Publications Relating to Home Economics & Human Nutrition 88
A 77.706:	Regulations, Rules, & Instructions Relating to Home Economics & Human Nutrition 88–A
A 77.708:	Family Economics Review 88–B
A 77.710:	Nutrition Program News 88–C

Agricultural Stabilization and Conservation Service

A 82.2:	General Publications 106
A 82.5:	Laws 107
A 82.6:	Regulations, Rules, & Instructions 110
A 82.6/4:	Handbooks, Manuals, Guides 106–A
	Agriculture Conservation Program:
A 82.37:	——Handbooks by States 103–A–1 to 103–A–50
A 82.37:M32/	——Maps 103–B
A 82.37:Su6/	——Summaries 103–B
A 82.37/3:	Statistical Summaries (various commodity programs) 103–B
A 82.79/2:	Conservation Reserve Program of Soil Bank, Statistical Summaries 104–A

Commodity Credit Corporation

A 82.301:	Annual Report 34
A 82.302:	General Publications 35
A 82.305:	Laws 36
A 82.306:	Regulations, Rules, & Instructions 37
A 82.311:	Charts Providing Graphic Summary of Operations 34–A

Farmers Home Administration

A 84.2:	General Publications 68
A 84.6:	Regulations, Rules, & Instructions 69
A 84.6/2:	Handbooks, Manuals, Guides 68–A

Commodity Exchange Authority

A 85.2:	General Publications 39
A 85.6:	Regulations, Rules, & Instructions 40
A 85.16:	Market Survey Report 39–A

Agricultural Marketing Service

A 88.2:	General Publications 24–B
A 88.5:	Laws 24–O
A 88.6:	Regulations, Rules, & Instructions 107–B
A 88.6/4:	Handbooks, Manuals, Guides 24–P
A 88.6/5:	USDA–C&MS Visual Aids 24–P
A 88.12/31:	Fresh Fruit and Vegetable Unloads FVUS (series) 19–A
A 88.14/12:	Dairy Plants Surveyed & Approved for USDA Grading Service 21–Q
A 88.15/23:	List of Plants Operating under USDA Poultry and Egg Inspection and Grading Programs 40–B–1
A 88.16/20:	Directory of Meat and Poultry Inspection Program 32–A
A 88.17/4:	Institutional Meat Purchase Specifications 24–N
A 88.17/7:	Federal Meat and Poultry Inspection Statistical Summary (annual) 21–S
A 88.17/8:	Meat and Poultry Inspection Program, Program Issuances 21–T
A 88.26/4:	Acreage-Marketing Guides 18–D
A 88.26/5:	PMG (series) 18–D
A 88.34:	Tobacco Stocks Reports 24–D
A 88.34/5:	Light Air-Cured Tobacco Market Review 24–D
A 88.34/6:	Flue-Cured Tobacco Market Review 24–D
A 88.34/8:	Fire-Cured & Dark Air-Cured Tobacco Market Review 24–D
A 88.43/2:	Plants Under USDA Continuous Inspection, Processed Fruits & Vegetables & Related Products 21–R

Farmer Cooperative Service

A 89.2:	General Publications 65–C
A 89.3:	Bulletins 63
A 89.4:	FCS Circulars 64
A 89.4/2:	FCS Educational Circulars 64
A 89.8:	News for Farmer Cooperatives 66
A 89.11:	General Reports 65–A
A 89.15:	Information (series) 65–B
A 89.19:	FCS Research Reports (numbered) 64–A

Statistical Reporting Service

A 92.2:	General Publications 122–A–1
A 92.9/3:	Chickens and Eggs, Farm Production, Disposition, etc. 21–F
A 92.10/2:	Milk, Production, Disposition, and Income 24–F
A 92.10/5:	Production of Manufactured Dairy Products 24–F
A 92.10/6:	Milk Production & Dairy Products (annual) 24–F
A 92.11/10:	Vegetables, Processing Vg 3–2 24–E
A 92.11/10–2:	Vegetables, Fresh Market Vg 2–2 24–E

5

Business Economics Office
(See also C 56.)

C 43.2:	General Publications 227–A
	Survey of Current Business
C 43.8/3:	——Special Supplements 228
C 43.8/4:	——Statistical Supplements 228

Economic Development Administration

C 46.1:	Annual Report 130–F
C 46.2:	General Publications 130–D
C 46.8:	Handbooks, Manuals, Guides 130–C
C 46.9/2:	Economic Development (monthly) 215–B
C 46.18:	Bibliographies and Lists of Publications 130–K
C 46.19/2:	Directory of Approved Projects 130–J
C 46.25:	Qualified Areas under Public Works and Economic Development Act of 1965, Public Law 89–136, Reports 130–J
C 46.25/2:	Areas Eligible for Financial Assistance under Public Works & Economic Development Act of 1965 130–J

United States Travel Service

C 47.1:	Annual Report 271–A
C 47.2:	General Publications 271–A–1
C 47.12:	Handbooks, Manuals, Guides 271–A–2
C 47.15/3:	Major Metropolitan Market Area (quarterly) 271–B
C 47.15/4:	Arrivals and Departures by Selected Ports (semi-annual) 271–A–3

National Technical Information Service

C 51.2:	General Publications 271
C 51.8:	Handbooks, Manuals, Guides 188–A–2
C 51.9:	Government Reports Index 270
C 51.9/3:	Government Reports Announcements 270
C 51.9/4:	Government Reports Index, Annual 270
C 51.11:	Bibliographies and Lists of Publications 188–A–1

Environmental Science Service Administration

C 52.13:	Monographs 208–B–3
C 52.25:	ESSA Science and Engineering (biennial) 208–B–12

Regional Economic Development Office

C 53.9:	Bibliographies and Lists of Publications 269–A–1

Foreign Direct Investments Office

C 54.2:	General Publications 232–E–1
C 54.6:	Regulations, Rules, and Instructions 232–E

National Oceanic and Atmospheric Administration

C 55.2:	General Publications 250–E–2
C 55.6:	Regulations, Rules, and Instructions 250–E–6
C 55.11:	Monthly Weather Review 277
C 55.12:	Federal Coordinator for Meteorological Services and Supporting Research, FCM (series) 250–E
C 55.13:	NOAA Technical Reports 208–B–7
C 55.13/2:	NOAA Technical Memorandums 208–B–7
C 55.14:	NOAA (quarterly) 250–E–1
C 55.15:	NOAA Program Plans (numbered) 250–E–3
C 55.16:	Federal Plan for Marine Environmental Prediction 250–E–2
C 55.16/2:	Federal Plan for Meterological Services and Supporting Research (annual) 208–B–4
C 55.17:	NOAA Publications Announcements 250–E–5
C 55.19:	NOAA Photoessays (numbered) 250–E–7
C 55.20:	Natural Disaster Survey Reports (numbered) 250–E–8
C 55.22:	NOAA Atlases (numbered) 250–E–9
C 55.25:	ESSA Professional Papers 208–B–6

National Weather Service

C 55.102:	General Publications 275
C 55.106:	Regulations, Rules, and Instructions 278–A
C 55.108:	Handbooks, Manuals, Guides 275–E
C 55.108/2:	Weather Service Observing Handbooks 275–E
C 55.109:	Average Monthly Weather Outlook 275–F
C 55.111:	Operations of National Weather Service 278–B
C 55.117:	Daily River Stages 274
C 55.119:	Weather Service of Merchant Shipping 282–A
C 55.120:	Hydrometeorological Reports 275–A

Environmental Data Service

C 55.202:	General Publications 273–D–1
C 55.210:	Mariners Weather Log (bimonthly) 275–D
C 55.214/49:	Climatological Data for Arctic Stations 273–D
C 55.214/50:	Climatological Data for Antarctic Stations 273–D
C 55.219:	Key to Meteorological Records Documentation 275–C
C 55.220/2:	World Data Center A, Oceanography: Catalogue of Accessioned Soviet Publications 834–N–2
C 55.220/3:	World Data Center A, Oceanography: Oceanographic Data Exchange 834–N–2
C 55.220/4:	World Data Center A, Oceanography: Publications (unnumbered) 834–N–2
C 55.221:	Climatography of United States 60-nos., Climates of States 273–B
C 55.221/2:	Decennial Census of U.S. Climate 279–A
C 55.224:	Lists of the Periodicals in the Collections of Atmospheric Sciences Library and Marine and Earth Sciences Library 273–D–2

National Marine Fisheries Service

C 55.302:	General Publications 609–C–1
C 55.309:	Frozen Fish Reports, Preliminary (Non-GPO) 610–A
C 55.309/2:	Current Fisheries Statistics 610–A
C 55.309/3:	Industrial Fishery Products Situation and Outlook 610–A
C 55.309/4:	Shellfish, Situation and Outlook 610–A
C 55.309/5:	Foodfish, Situation and Outlook 610–A
C 55.310:	Commercial Fisheries Review (monthly) 609–A
C 55.310/2:	Commercial Fisheries Abstracts (monthly) 609–B
C 55.313:	Fishery Bulletin 611
C 55.314:	Fishery Leaflets 611–D
C 55.316:	Statistical Digest (series) 615

National Ocean Survey

C 55.402:	General Publications 192
C 55.408:	Handbooks, Manuals, Guides 192–B
C 55.412:	Preliminary Determination of Epicenters (monthly) 192–C
C 55.413:	Bibliographies and Lists of Publications 207–A–1
C 55.417/2:	United States Earthquakes (annual) 208
C 55.419:	NOS Publications (numbered) 193
C 55.420:	Great Lakes Pilot 338
C 55.421:	Tide Tables, High and Low Water Predictions, West Coast of North and South America and including Hawaiian Islands 199
C 55.421/2:	Tide Tables, High and Low Water Predictions, East Coast of North and South America, Including Greenland 197
C 55.421/3:	Tide Tables, High and Low Water Predictions, Europe and West Coast of Africa, including Mediterranean Sea 198

171 404 O - 72 - 2

D 119.8/5:	Technical Memorandums 320–B–7
D 119.8/6:	Professional Manuals PM (series) 320–B–3
D 119.8/7:	Instructor's Guide IG (series) 857–D–12
D 119.8/8:	Student Manuals SM (series) 320–B–1
D 119.9:	Technical Report TR (series) 320–B–2
D 119.11:	Miscellaneous Publications MP (series) 857–D–11
D 119.13:	Leaflets L (series) 857–D–5
D 119.14:	Buildings with Fallout Protection, Design Case Studies 320–B–8
D 119.15:	HS–(series) 320–B–9

Provost Marshal General

D 120.8:	Handbooks, Manuals, Guides 362–A

NAVY DEPARTMENT

D 201.2:	General Publications 370
D 201.5:	Laws 371
D 201.6:	Regulations, Rules, & Instructions 373
D 201.6/10:	Navy Procurement Directives 373
D 201.6/10–2:	Navy Procurement Directives, Supplements 373
D 201.6/11:	Index to Navy Procurement Information 373
D 201.6/12:	Handbooks, Manuals, Guides 370–A
D 201.9:	Your Navy, from the Viewpoint of the Nation's Finest Artists 373–B
D 201.11:	Navy Regulations 372
D 201.14:	Navy Management Review 371–A
D 201.15:	United States Antarctica Program (annual report) 373–A
D 201.15/2:	Naval Support Force, Antarctica: Publications 373–A
D 201.15/3:	Naval Support Force, Antarctica: Monograph (series) 373–A
D 201.17:	Direction (monthly) 369–B
D 201.20:	MC Reports, Issued by Maury Center for Ocean Sciences (numbered) 370–B

Naval Air Systems Command

D 202.2:	General Publications 374 (Rev.)
D 202.6/7:	Handbooks, Manuals, Guides 374–B (Rev.)
D 202.9:	Naval Aviation News 375
D 202.13:	Approach 374–A
D 202.19:	Mech (quarterly) 374–D
D 202.20:	Fathom 374–A–1

Naval Oceanographic Office

D 203.1:	Annual Report 377–A (Rev. 1964)
D 203.2:	General Publications 377
D 203.22:	Publications (numbered) 378 (Rev. 1957)
D 203.22/3:	Special Publications SP–(series) 377–C
D 203.24:	National Oceanographic Data Center Publications (numbered) 377–D
D 203.31:	Global Ocean Floor Analysis and Research Data Series 377–E

Civilian Manpower Management Office

D 204.6:	Regulations, Rules, & Instructions 378–A
D 204.6/2:	Handbooks, Manuals, Guides 378–B
D 204.7:	Safety Review 379
D 204.9:	Journal of Navy Civilian Personnel Management (quarterly) 369–C

Judge Advocate General

D 205.2:	General Publications 380
D 205.6:	Regulations, Rules, & Instructions 382–A
D 205.6/2:	Handbooks, Manuals, Guides 380–A
D 205.7:	JAG Journal 381
D 205.8:	Laws 382
D 205.9:	Federal Income Tax Information for Armed Forces Personnel (annual) 380–B

Medicine and Surgery Bureau

D 206.2:	General Publications 385
D 206.6:	Regulations, Rules, & Instructions 387
D 206.6/3:	Handbooks, Manuals, Guides 385–B
D 206.11:	Medical Statistics of U.S. Navy 388
D 206.12:	History of Medical Department of Navy, World War II 385–A
D 206.15:	Statistics of Navy Medicine 388–A

Naval Operations Office

D 207.2:	General Publications 399
D 207.6:	Regulations, Rules, & Instructions 400
D 207.6/2:	Handbooks, Manuals, Guides 399–C
D 207.10:	History of Ships of American Navy 399–A
D 207.10/2:	Historical Publications 399–A
D 207.11:	Bibliographies and Lists of Publications 399–B
D 207.12:	Naval Documents of the American Revolution 399–D
D 207.13:	Shipbuilding and Conversion Program (annual) 400–A

Naval Personnel Bureau

D 208.2:	General Publications 403
D 208.3:	All Hands 401
D 208.6:	Regulations, Rules, & Instructions 406
D 208.6/2:	Bureau of Naval Personnel Manual 403–A
D 208.6/3:	Handbooks, Manuals, Guides 403–A
D 208.7:	Naval Training Bulletin 402
D 208.11:	Rate Training Manuals 404
D 208.11/2:	Navy Training Text Material 404
D 208.11/3:	Navy Life, Reading and Writing for Success in Navy 404
D 208.12:	Register of Commissioned and Warrant Officers of the U.S. Navy & Marine Corps & Reserve Officers on Active Duty 405
D 208.12/2:	Naval Reserve Register 405
D 208.12/3:	Register of Retired Commissioned and Warrant Officers Regular and Reserve, of the Navy and Marine Corps 405
D 208.13:	Case Instruction Series 402–A
D 208.15:	Bibliographies and Lists of Publications 401–A

Naval Academy

D 208.102:	General Publications 391
D 208.107:	Annual Register 389
D 208.108:	Admission Regulations 392
D 208.109:	Catalogue of Information 390–A

Naval War College, Newport

D 208.207:	International Law Studies 408–A
D 208.207/2:	——Indexes 408–A

Naval Facilities Engineering Command

D 209.2:	General Publications 418
D 209.10:	Technical Publications (numbered) 419–A
D 209.13:	Navy Civil Engineer (bimonthly) 419–B
D 209.14:	Handbooks, Manuals, Guides 418–A
D 209.14/2:	Design Manuals 418–A
D 209.15:	Index of Publications 418–B

Naval Research Office

D 210.2:	General Publications 407
D 210.6:	Regulations, Rules, & Instructions 408
D 210.6/2:	Handbooks, Manuals, Guides 407–F
D 210.11:	Naval Research Reviews 407–C
D 210.12:	Naval Research Logistics Quarterly 407–B
D 210.15:	ONR Report DR-series 407–D

Naval Ship Systems Command

D 211.2:	General Publications 412
D 211.6:	Regulations, Rules, & Instructions 414
D 211.6/2:	Handbooks, Manuals, Guides 412–B
D 211.9:	Naval Ship Research and Development Center Reports 412–C
D 211.22:	Faceplate (quarterly) 412–D

Naval Supply Systems Command

D 212.2:	General Publications 415
D 212.6:	Regulations, Rules, & Instructions 417
D 212.6/3:	Handbooks, Manuals, Guides 415–B
D 212.15:	Bibliographies & Lists of Publications 415–C

Naval Observatory

D 213.2:	General Publications 397
D 213.7:	Air Almanac 393
D 213.8:	American Ephemeris and Nautical Almanac 394
D 213.8/3:	Astronomical Phenomena 396–A
D 213.9:	Astronomical Papers 396
D 213.10:	Publications (2d series) 398
D 213.11:	Nautical Almanac 395

Marine Corps

D 214.2:	General Publications 383
D 214.6:	Regulations, Rules, and Instructions 384–C
D 214.9/2:	Handbooks, Manuals, Guides 384
D 214.9/3:	Technical Manuals 384
D 214.9/4:	Fleet Marine Force Manuals, FMFM (series) 384
D 214.10:	Reserve Marine (monthly) 384–A
D 214.12:	Regimental and Squadron Histories 384–B
D 214.13:	Historical Publications 383–B

Naval Ordnance Systems Command

D 215.6/2:	Handbooks, Manuals, Guides 409–A
D 215.9:	Ordnance Pamphlets OP (series) 410–A

Military Sea Transportation Service

D 216.8:	Sealift Magazine (monthly) 388–B–1

Oceanographer of the Navy

D 218.2:	General Publications 377

Naval Electronic Systems Command

D 219.8:	Handbooks, Manuals, Guides 414–A

AIR FORCE DEPARTMENT

D 301.2:	General Publications 424
D 301.6/2:	Regulations, Rules, & Instructions 425
D 301.6/4:	Air Force Procurement Instructions 425
D 301.6/5:	Handbooks, Manuals, Guides 424–F
D 301.7:	Air Force Manuals 421
D 301.7/4:	Civil Air Patrol Manuals 421
D 301.7/5:	AACS Manuals 421
D 301.7/6:	MAC Manuals 421
D 301.8:	Air Reservist 422
D 301.26:	Air University Review 422–A
D 301.27:	Air Weather Service Manuals 421
D 301.35:	Air Force Pamphlets 421–A
D 301.35/3:	Air Force Systems Command Pamphlets AFSCP 421–A
D 301.38/4:	The Navigator 424–C
D 301.38/7:	Instructors' Journal 424–G
D 301.44:	Aerospace Safety 423–A
D 301.45:	Air Force Systems Command Publications 422–B
D 301.45/14:	Air Force Systems Command Manual AFSCM 421
D 301.45/14–2:	AFSCR (Air Force Systems Command Regulations) (series) 421
D 301.45/19–2:	Air Force Office of Scientific Research AFOSR Series 422–B
D 301.54:	Information Services Fact Sheets 424–D
D 301.56:	MAC Flyer 424–B
D 301.60:	Airman (monthly) 422–D
D 301.62/2:	Bibliographies and Lists of Publications 424–I
D 301.65:	Air Force Civil Engineer (quarterly) 421–B
D 301.69/3:	OAR Series 422–B
D 301.69/5:	Office of Aerospace Research Publications 422–B
D 301.69/6–2:	Air Force Research Review 424–H
D 301.72:	Driver, Traffic Safety Magazine of United States Air Force 423–B
D 301 73:	The Air Force Comptroller (quarterly) 421–C
D 301.76/3:	Lithograph Series Catalog 421–E
D 301.78:	Proceedings of Military History Symposium 421–D

Judge Advocate General of Air Force

D 302.2:	General Publications 428
D 302.6:	Regulations, Rules, & Instructions 427–A
D 302.9:	Air Force JAG Law Review 427–B

Administrative Services

D 303.2:	General Publications 427
D 303.7:	Air Force Register 426

Air Force Medical Service

D 304.1:	Annual Reports 428–A
D 304.2:	General Publications 428–B

Air Force Academy

D 305.2:	General Publications 425–A–1
D 305.8:	U.S. Air Force Academy Catalog 425–A

Inspector General of Air Force

D 306.8:	Aerospace Maintenance Safety (monthly) 428–C

DISTRICT OF COLUMBIA
District Court of U.S. for D.C.

DC 21.9:	List of Legal Investments for Trust Funds in District of Columbia (semiannual) 430–A

Public Service Commission

DC 43.1:	Annual Report 430–A–2

National Capital Housing Authority

DC 57.	Reports and Publications 430–A–3

ENVIRONMENTAL PROTECTION AGENCY

EP 1.1:	Annual Report 431–I–4
EP 1.2:	General Publications 431–I–1
EP 1.3/2:	EPA Citizens' Bulletin 431–I–8
EP 1.5:	Laws 431–I–2
EP 1.8:	Handbooks, Manuals, Guides 431–I–5
EP 1.10:	Addresses 431–I–6
EP 1.11:	Comprehensive Studies of Solid Waste Management, Annual Report 431–I–3
EP 1.16:	Water Pollution Control Research Series 473–A–1
EP 1.16/2:	Proceedings, Conferences in Matter of Pollution of Navigable Waters 473–A–1
EP 1.17:	Solid Waste Management Series, SW-(numbered) 431–I–7
EP 1.18:	Accession Bulletin, Solid Waste Information Retrieval System (monthly) 487–A–7

Water Programs Office

EP 2.3/2:	Technical Bulletins 473–A–7
EP 2.5:	Laws 607–D
EP 2.8:	Handbooks, Manuals, Guides 607–C
EP 2.11:	Oil and Hazardous Substances Program Series 473–A–4
EP 2.12:	Research, Development, and Demonstration Projects, Grants and Contract Awards 473–A–3
EP 2.13:	Project Register, Distribution by River Basin of Projects Approved under Sec. 8 of Federal Water Pollution Control Act (Public Law 660, 84th Cong.) as amended 607–E
EP 2.14:	Cost of Clean Water [annual report to Congress] 473–A–2

EP 2.15:	Northwest Shellfish Sanitation Research Planning Conference, Proceedings 473-A-5
EP 2.17:	Inventory Municipal Waste Facilities, Cooperative State Reports 473-A-1
EP 2.19:	Estuarine Pollution Study Series 607-C-2
EP 2.20:	Sewage Facilities Construction (annual) 498-A
EP 2.21:	Digest of State Program Plans (fiscal year) 473-A-6
EP 2.24:	Fish Kills Caused by Pollution (annual) 496-C

Solid Waste Management Office

EP 3.5:	Laws 487-A-5
EP 3.8:	Handbooks, Manuals, Guides 487-A-2
EP 3.9:	Bibliographies and Lists of Publications 487-A-3
EP 3.10:	State Solid Waste Planning Grants, Agencies, and Progress Report of Activities 487-A-4
EP 3.12:	Solid Waste Management Training Bulletin of Courses 487-A-6

Air Programs Office

EP 4.2:	General Publications 483-E-1
EP 4.8:	Handbooks, Manuals, Guides 483-E-2
EP 4.9:	Air Programs Office Publication, AP-(series) 483-E
EP 4.9/2:	Air Programs Office Publication, APTD-(series) 483-E
EP 4.10:	Air Pollution Report, Federal Facilities 483-E
EP 4.11:	Air Pollution Abstracts 483-E-3
EP 4.12:	Addresses 483-E-4
EP 4.13:	Air Pollution Training Courses 483-E-6

Pesticides Office

EP 5.2:	General Publications 473-B-1
EP 5.8:	Handbooks, Manuals, Guides 473-B-2
EP 5.9:	Health Aspects of Pesticides Abstract Bulletin 475-M

Radiation Office

EP 6.9:	Radiological Health Data and Reports (monthly) 498-B
EP 6.10:	RO/EERL [Eastern Environmental Radiation Laboratory] (series) 498-B-3
EP 6.10/2:	ORP/SID [Surveillance and Inspection Division] (series) 483-M

Technology Transfer

| EP 7.2: | General Publications 473-C-1 |

FINE ARTS COMMISSION

| FA 1. | Reports and Publications 432 |

FARM CREDIT ADMINISTRATION

FCA 1.1:	Annual Report 430-J-1
FCA 1.2:	General Publications 430-J-2
FCA 1.3:	Bulletins 430-J-3
FCA 1.4:	Circulars (numbered) 430-J-4
FCA 1.4/2:	——(letter-numbers) 430-J-4

FEDERAL HOME LOAN BANK BOARD

FHL 1.1:	Annual Report 595
FHL 1.2:	General Publications 596
FHL 1.6:	Regulations, Rules, & Instructions 597
FHL 1.6/2:	Handbooks, Manuals, Guides 597
FHL 1.27:	Journal of Federal Home Loan Bank Board (monthly) 597-A

FEDERAL MEDIATION AND CONCILIATION SERVICE

| FM 1.1: | Annual Report 433 |
| FM 1.2: | General Publications 434 |

FEDERAL MARITIME COMMISSION

FMC 1.1:	Annual Report 233
FMC 1.2:	General Publications 432-L-1
FMC 1.6:	Regulations, Rules, and Instructions 237
FMC 1.10:	Reports (decisions) 233-A
FMC 1.11:	Approved Conference, Rate & Interconference Agreements of Steamship Lines in Foreign Commerce of United States 432-L

FEDERAL POWER COMMISSION

FP 1.1:	Annual Report 435
FP 1.2:	General Publications 436
FP 1.5:	Laws 437
FP 1.6:	Rules of Practice & Procedure 439
FP 1.7:	Regulations, Rules, & Instructions 439
FP 1.7/2:	Uniform Systems of Accounts Prescribed for Natural Gas Companies 439
FP 1.10:	FPC R [Rate] (series) 438-A
FP 1.12:	FPC P [Power] (series) 435-D
FP 1.18:	National Electric Rate Book [by States] 437-A-1 to 437-A-50
FP 1.20:	Opinions & Decisions 438
FP 1.21:	FPC S [Statistics] (series) 440
FP 1.27:	Electric Power Statistics 435-E

FEDERAL RESERVE SYSTEM BOARD OF GOVERNORS

FR 1.2:	General Publications 442
FR 1.6:	Regulations, Rules, & Instructions 443
FR 1.8/3:	Handbooks, Manuals, Guides 443

FEDERAL TRADE COMMISSION

FT 1.1:	Annual Report 533
FT 1.2:	General Publications [Includes Economic Reports] 535
FT 1.3/2:	Consumer Bulletins 533-A
FT 1.7:	Rules of Practice 538
FT 1.8:	Regulations, Rules, & Instructions 537
FT 1.8/2:	Handbooks, Manuals, Guides 535-A
FT 1.11:	FTC Decisions 534
FT 1.12/2:	Advisory Opinion Digest 534-A
FT 1.13:	Statutes & Decisions (court) 539
FT 1.13/2:	——Supplements 539
FT 1.18:	Quarterly Financial Report, U.S. Mfg. Corporations 536-A

FOREIGN-TRADE ZONES BOARD

FTZ 1.1:	Annual Report 542
FTZ 1.2:	General Publications 542
FTZ 1.5:	Laws 542

GENERAL ACCOUNTING OFFICE

GA 1.1:	Annual Report 543
GA 1.2:	General Publications 545
GA 1.5:	Decisions of Comptroller General 544
GA 1.5/3:	Index-Digest of Published Decisions of Comptroller General 546
GA 1.12:	Joint Financial Management Improvement Program (annual report) 546-A
GA 1.14:	Handbooks, Manuals, Guides 545-A
GA 1.15:	GAO Review 544-A (Rev.)

GOVERNMENT PRINTING OFFICE

GP 1.2:	General Publications 548
GP 1.23/4:	Handbooks, Manuals, Guides 548
GP 1.26:	Apprentice Training Series 548

Public Documents Department

GP 3.2:	General Publications 551
GP 3.7/2:	Numerical Lists and Schedule of Volumes 553
GP 3.8:	Monthly Catalog 557
GP 3.9:	Price Lists 554
GP 3.17:	Selected United States Government Publications 556
GP 3.22:	Lists of Publications (miscellaneous) 552

GENERAL SERVICES ADMINISTRATION

GS 1.1:	Annual Report 558
GS 1.2:	General Publications 559
GS 1.5:	Laws 560
GS 1.6/5:	Federal Procurement Regulations, FPR Circulars 558–A
GS 1.6/6:	Handbooks, Manuals, Guides 559–B
GS 1.6/6–2:	Counseling Guides (numbered) 558–A–1
GS 1.15:	Inventory Report on Real Property Owned by United States Throughout the World 559–A
GS 1.15/2:	Inventory Report on Real Property Leased to United States Throughout the World 559–A
GS 1.15/3:	Inventory Report on Legislative Jurisdiction over Federal Areas 559–A
GS 1.17:	Bibliographies and Lists of Publications 559
GS 1.19:	Consumer Information Series 558–A–2

Federal Supply Service

GS 2.2:	General Publications 564
GS 2.6:	Regulations, Rules, & Instructions 565–A
GS 2.6/3:	Handbooks, Manuals, Guides 564–A
GS 2.6/4:	Scientific Inventory Management Series 564–A
GS 2.8:	Federal Specifications 563
GS 2.8/2:	Index of Federal Specifications & Standards 565
GS 2.8/3:	Federal Standards 563
GS 2.8/7:	Federal Test Method Standards 563
GS 2.10/5:	Federal Stock Number Reference Catalog 565–D
GS 2.10/6:	GSA Stock Catalog 565–B
GS 2.10/7:	National Supplier Change Index Series 565–B
GS 2.15:	Inventory of Automatic Data Processing Equipment in U.S. Government 853–B

National Archives and Records Service

GS 4.2:	General Publications 569
GS 4.6:	Regulations, Rules, & Instructions 570
GS 4.6/2:	Handbooks, Manuals, Guides 569–B
GS 4.13:	Territorial Papers of U.S. 571
GS 4.14:	National Historical Publications Commission, Publications 569–A
GS 4.17:	Publications (list) 569–C
GS 4.17/2:	List of National Archives Microfilm Publications 569–C
GS 4.21:	Military Operations of Civil War, Guide-Index to Official Records of Union and Confederate Armies, 1861–1865 569–D
GS 4.22:	General Information Leaflet Series 569
GS 4.24:	Directory of U.S. Government Audiovisual Personnel 567–B

Federal Register Office

GS 4.102:	General Publications 574
GS 4.107:	Federal Register (daily) 573
GS 4.108:	Code of Federal Regulations & Supplements 572
GS 4.108/2:	——Title 3, Supplements 572
GS 4.109:	U.S. Gov't Organization Manual 577
GS 4.110:	Slip Laws (public) 575
GS 4.111:	Statutes at Large 576
GS 4.111/2:	Statutes at Large, Tables of Laws Affected 576
GS 4.113:	Public Papers of Presidents of United States (annual) 574–A
GS 4.114:	Weekly Compilation of Presidential Documents 577–A

Public Buildings Service

GS 6.2:	General Publications 579
GS 6.6:	Regulations, Rules, & Instructions 580
GS 6.6/2:	Handbooks, Manuals, Guides 580
GS 6.8:	Historical Studies 579–A

Transportation and Communications Service

GS 8.2:	General Publications 580–A–1
GS 8.6/2:	Handbooks, Manuals, Guides 580–A

Consumer Product Information Coordinating Center

GS 11.9:	Consumer Product Information Index of Selected Federal Publications of Consumer Interest 580–B

HEALTH, EDUCATION, AND WELFARE DEPARTMENT

HE 1.1:	Annual Report 444
HE 1.2:	General Publications 445
HE 1.6:	Regulations, Rules, & Instructions 445–A
HE 1.6/3:	Handbooks, Manuals, Guides 445–A
HE 1.6/6:	Catalog of HEW Assistance Providing Financial Support and Service to States, Communities, Organizations, Individuals (annual) 445–A
HE 1.6/7:	Grants Administration Manual 445–A
HE 1.6/7–2:	Grants Administration Manual Circulars 445–A
HE 1.7:	Addresses 445–I
HE 1.10:	Training Manuals 447
HE 1.17:	Field Directory (annual) 444–D
HE 1.18:	Bibliographies and Lists of Publications 444–B
HE 1.18/3:	Catalog, U.S. Department of Health, Education, and Welfare Publications 444–B
HE 1.19:	Health, Education, and Welfare Trends (annual) 445–B
HE 1.21:	HEW Facts and Figures 445–F
HE 1.23:	Proposed Mental Retardation Programs 445–G
HE 1.23/3:	Mental Retardation Grants 445–G
HE 1.23/5:	Mental Retardation Activities of Department of Health, Education, and Welfare 445–G
HE 1.26:	Education and Training, Annual Report of Secretary of Health, Education, and Welfare to Congress on Training Activities under Manpower Development and Training Act 444–C
HE 1.29:	Program Analysis (series) 445–H
HE 1.32:	Task Force on Prescription Drugs Publications 445
HE 1.33:	Report of Career Service Board for Science 445–K
HE 1.36:	Project Head Start 857–H–12
HE 1.37:	Footnote 445–M
HE 1.38:	Directory of Public Elementary and Secondary Schools in Selected Districts Enrollment and Staff by Racial/Ethnic Group 444–B–1
HE 1.39:	Progress Report on Nurse Training, Report to the President and the Congress 445–H–1
HE 1.40:	Health Professions Educational Assistance Program, Report to the President and the Congress 445–D–1
HE 1.41:	DHEW Obligations to [various institutions] 444–E

Facilities Engineering and Construction Agency

HE 1.109:	Representative Construction Costs of Hospitals and Related Health Facilities (semi-annual) 486–A–1

Social Security Administration

HE 3.2:	General Publications 516
HE 3.3:	Social Security Bulletin 523
HE 3.3/3:	——Statistical Supplements (annual) 523
HE 3.4:	Information Service Circulars 517
HE 3.5:	Laws 518
HE 3.6:	Regulations, Rules, & Instructions 520

HE 3.6/3:	Handbooks, Manuals, Guides 516–C
HE 3.6/4:	Health Insurance for the Aged, HIM (series) 516–C
HE 3.25/2:	Amendments to Social Security Laws, SSI–date–nos. 527–A
HE 3.33:	International Technical Cooperation Series 517–A
HE 3.38:	Bibliographies and Lists of Publications 516–B
HE 3.40:	Annual Statistics on Workers Under Social Security 516–A
HE 3.41:	Report of Advisory Council on Social Security Financing 520–A
HE 3.44:	Social Security Rulings on Old-Age, Survivors and Disability Insurance 523–A
HE 3.44/2:	Social Security Rulings, Cum. Bulletins 523–A
HE 3.49:	Research Reports 522–A
HE 3.51/5:	Directory, Medicare Providers and Suppliers of Services, Hospitals, Extended Care Facilities, Home Health Agencies, etc. 515–A
HE 3.52:	Social Security Information SSI (series) 523–B
HE 3.52/2:	TIB [Technical Information Bulletin] (series) 523–C
HE 3.57:	Health Insurance for the Aged (annual) 516–D

Education Office

HE 5.2:	General Publications 461(Rev. 1965)
HE 5.6:	Regulations, Rules, and Instructions 461–A (Rev.)
HE 5.6/2:	Handbooks, Manuals, Guides 461–A (Rev. 1965)
HE 5.8:	Addresses 455–C
HE 5.10:	Bibliographies and Lists of Publications 455–D
HE 5.25:	Education Directory 460
HE 5.75:	American Education (10 times yearly) 455–B
HE 5.77:	Research in Education (monthly) 466–A
HE 5.79:	Title 1, Elementary and Secondary Education Act of 1965, States Report (annual) 467–D
HE 5.80:	Status of Compliance, Public School Districts, 17 Southern and Border States, Report (monthly) 467–C
HE 5.81:	Higher Education Reports 462–A
HE 5.82:	Report on Cooperative Research to Improve the Nation's Schools (annual) 467–E
HE 5.83:	Composite List of Eligible Institutions For Guaranteed Loans for College Students: Higher Education Act of 1965 459–A
HE 5.83/2:	——National Vocational Student Loan Insurance Act of 1965 459–A
HE 5.84:	Institute Programs for Advanced Study 460–A–58
HE 5.85:	National Advisory Council on Vocational Education Annual Report 462–B
HE 5.86:	National Advisory Committee on Handicapped Children Annual Report 461–B
HE 5.88:	Focus on Follow Through 461
HE 5.89:	PREP Reports (numbered) 461–C
	Miscellaneous publications:
HE 5.210:	—General OE 10,000–10,999 460–A–10
HE 5.211:	—Publications about OE and HEW, OE 11,000–11,999 460–A–11
HE 5.212:	—Research, OE 12,000–12,999 460–A–12
HE 5.213:	—Adult Education, OE 13,000–13,999 460–A–13
HE 5.214:	—International Education, OE 14,000–14,999 460–A–14
HE 5.215:	—Library Services, OE 15,000–15,999 460–A–15
HE 5.216:	—Nursery Schools and Kindergartens, OE 16,000–16,999 460–A–16
	Elementary and Secondary Education publications:
HE 5.220:	—Misc. General Statistics, OE 20,000–20,999 460–A–20
HE 5.221:	—Buildings, equipment, OE 21,000–21,999 460–A–21
HE 5.222:	—Finances, receipts, expenditures, OE 22,000–22,999 460–A–22
HE 5.223:	—Administration, faculties, salaries, OE 23,000–23,999 460–A–23
HE 5.224:	—Enrollment, retention, graduates, OE 24,000–24,999 460–A–24
HE 5.225:	—Guidance, testing, counseling, OE 25,000–25,999 460–A–25
HE 5.226:	—Careers, OE 26,000–26,999 460–A–26
HE 5.227:	—Foreign languages, OE 27,000–27,999 460–A–27
HE 5.228:	—Health, physical education, recreation, OE 28,000–28,999 460–A–28
HE 5.229:	—Mathematics, science, OE 29,000–29,999 460–A–29
HE 5.230:	—Language, arts, reading, writing, speaking, OE 30,000–30,999 460–A–30
HE 5.231:	—Social studies, OE 31,000–31,999 460–A–31
HE 5.232:	—Curriculums, subjects, activities (elementary only), OE 32,000–32,999 460–A–32
HE 5.233:	—Curriculums, subjects, activities (secondary & elementary-secondary), OE 33,000–33,999 460–A–33
HE 5.234:	—Audio-visual, OE 34,000–34,999 460–A–34
HE 5.235:	—Special education, exceptional children, OE 35,000–35,999 460–A–35
HE 5.236:	—Rural schools, rural education, OE 36,000–36,999 460–A–36
HE 5.237:	—Education of the Disadvantaged, OE 37,000–37,999 460–A–37
HE 5.238:	—Equal Educational Opportunities, OE 38,000–38,999 460–A–38
	Higher Education publications:
HE 5.250:	—Miscellaneous, general statistics, OE 50,000–50,999 460–A–50
HE 5.251:	—Buildings, equipment, OE 51,000–51,999 460–A–51
HE 5.252:	—Finance, receipts, expenditures, OE 52,000–52,999 460–A–52
HE 5.253:	—Administration, faculties, salaries, OE 53,000–53,999 460–A–53
HE 5.254:	—Admission, enrollment, retention, degrees, graduates, OE 54,000–54,999 460–A–54
HE 5.255:	—Student financial assistance, OE 55,000–55,999 460–A–55
HE 5.256:	—Courses of study, subjects, OE 56,000–56,999 460–A–56
HE 5.257:	—Junior colleges, community colleges, post high school courses, OE 57,000–57,999 460–A–57
HE 5.258:	—Teacher education, OE 58,000–58,999 460–A–58
	Vocational Education publications:
HE 5.280:	—Miscellaneous, OE 80,000–80,999 460–A–80
HE 5.281:	—Agricultural education, OE 81,000–81,999 460–A–81
HE 5.282:	—Distributive education, OE 82,000–82,999 460–A–82
HE 5.283:	—Home economics education, OE 83,000–83,999 460–A–83

HE 5.284:	—Trade and industrial education, OE 84,-000–84,999 460–A–84
HE 5.285:	—Practical nurse education, OE 85,000–85,999 460–A–85
HE 5.286:	—"Office" Education, OE 86,000–86,999 460–A–86 *NOTE.*—Pertains to training in office work. Do not confuse with Office of Education, HEW.
HE 5.287:	—Manpower Development and Training, OE 87,000–87,999 460–A–87

Social and Rehabilitation Service

HE 17.2:	General Publications 512–A–1
HE 17.6:	Regulations, Rules, & Instructions 512–A–3
HE 17.8:	Handbooks, Manuals, Guides 512–A–3
HE 17.8/2:	Manuals for Volunteer Probation Programs 512–A–4
HE 17.14:	Addresses 532–A–6
HE 17.15:	Social and Rehabilitation Service Research and Demonstration Projects 512–A–2
HE 17.16:	Parole Series 532–A–7
HE 17.16/2:	Correction Series 532–A–7
HE 17.16/3:	Legal Series 532–A–7
HE 17.16/4:	Studies in Delinquency 532–A–7
HE 17.17:	Bibliographies and Lists of Publications 532–A–3
HE 17.19:	Public Assistance Reports 519
HE 17.20:	National Citizens Conference on Rehabilitation of the Disabled and Disadvantaged 532–A–8
HE 17.23:	Statistical Series (numbered) 454
HE 17.24:	Working Papers (numbered) 532–A–10
HE 17.25:	Research Reports (numbered) 532–A–11

Rehabilitation Services Administration

HE 17.102:	General Publications 529
HE 17.106:	Regulations, Rules, and Instructions 530
HE 17.108:	Handbooks, Manuals, Guides 529–B
HE 17.109:	Rehabilitation Record 530–A
HE 17.110/3:	Rehabilitation Service Series 531
HE 17.112:	Bibliographies and Lists of Publications 528–A
HE 17.113:	Mental Retardation Abstracts 506–C–1
HE 17.119:	State Vocational Rehabilitation Agency Program Data, Fiscal Year 506–C–2
HE 17.119/2:	State Vocational Rehabilitation Agency: Fact Sheet Booklet 506–C–2

Aging Administration

HE 17.302:	General Publications 447–A–1
HE 17.308:	Handbooks, Manuals, Guides 447–A–3
HE 17.309:	Aging 444–A
HE 17.310:	Designs for Action for Older Americans 447–A–5
HE 17.311:	Bibliographies and Lists of Publications 447–A–6
HE 17.312:	Addresses 447–A–2
HE 17.313:	Patterns for Progress in Aging 447–A–3

Assistance Payments Administration

HE 17.402:	General Publications 512–B–2
HE 17.408:	Handbooks, Manuals, Guides 512–B–1

Medical Services Administration

HE 17.502:	General Publications 512–C
HE 17.508:	Handbooks, Manuals, Guides 512–C–1

National Center for Social Statistics

HE 17.602:	General Publications 512–D–3
HE 17.612:	Trend Report: Graphic Presentation of Public Assistance and Related Data, NCSS Report A–4 512–B
HE 17.614:	Program Facts on Federally Aided Public Assistance Income Maintenance Programs, NCSS Report A–6 512–D–1

HE 17.616:	Medical Assistance Financed under the Public Assistance Titles of the Social Security Act, NCSS Report B–1 512–D–4
HE 17.617/2:	Recipients and Amounts of Medical Vendor Payments under Public Assistance Programs, NCSS Report B–3 512–D–6
HE 17.617/3:	Number of Recipients and Amounts of Payment under Medicaid and Other Medical Programs Financed from Public Assistance Funds, NCSS Report B–4 512–D–2
HE 17.621:	Medicaid and other Medical Care Financed from Public Assistance Funds, NCSS Report B–6 512–D–2
HE 17.638:	Child Welfare Statistics, NCSS Report CW–1 512–D
HE 17.639/3:	Report of Findings, AFDC Study NCSS Report AFDC–3 512–D–5
HE 17.640:	NCSS Report, H–(nos.) 512–D–7

Community Service Administration

HE 17.702:	General Publications 532–B–1
HE 17.708:	Handbooks, Manuals, Guides 532–B–3
HE 17.709:	Services to AFDC Families, Annual Report to Congress 532–B–2

Youth Development and Delinquency Prevention Administration

HE 17.802:	General Publications 532–C–2
HE 17.808:	Handbooks, Manuals, Guides 532–C–3
HE 17.809:	Bibliographies and Lists of Publications 532–C–4
HE 17.811:	Grants, Juvenile Delinquency Prevention Control Act 532–A–9

Public Health Service

HE 20.2:	General Publications 485
HE 20.5:	Laws 495–A
HE 20.6:	Regulations, Rules, & Instructions 499
HE 20.8:	Handbooks, Manuals, Guides 496–A
HE 20.10:	Health Information Series (numbered) 486
HE 20.11:	Public Health Service Bibliography Series 481–A
HE 20.13:	CCPM Pamphlets 483–I
HE 20.14:	Conference of State Sanitary Engineers, Report of Proceedings 494–A

Occupational Safety and Health Bureau

HE 20.1602:	General Publications 499–F–2
HE 20.1608:	Handbooks, Manuals, Guides 499–F–1

Community Environmental Management Bureau

HE 20.1810:	Community Environmental Management Series 468–A–7
HE 20.1811:	Environmental Health Services Series on Community Organization Techniques 512–F–1

Health Services and Mental Health Administration

HE 20.2002:	General Publications 483–T–1
HE 20.2008:	Handbooks, Manuals, Guides 483–T–2
HE 20.2010/2:	Health Services Report 497
HE 20.2011:	HSMHA Public Advisory Committees: Authority, Structure, Functions 483–T
HE 20.2011/2:	HSMHA Public Advisory Committees: Roster of Members 483–T
HE 20.2012:	List of Publications 481–A
HE 20.2012/2:	Bibliographies and Lists of Publications 483–T–4
HE 20.2013:	Emergency Health Series 486–E
HE 20.2013/2:	Emergency Health Services Digest 483–R
HE 20.2014:	Indian Health Program (annual) 483–T–3
HE 20.2014/2:	To the First Americans, Annual Report on Indian Health Program of Public Health Service 486–I
HE 20.2015:	Directory of Local Health and Mental Health Units 483–C

HE 20.2015/2:	Directory of State, Territorial, and Regional Health Authorities (annual) 483–B
HE 20.2016:	Grants-in-Aid and Other Financial Assistance Programs, HSMHA 483–P
HE 20.2018:	Monographs (numbered series) 500–A
HE 20.2019:	The Health Consequences of Smoking 485–A

National Center for Health Services Research and Development

HE 20.2102:	General Publications 491–B–1
HE 20.2108:	Handbooks, Manuals, Guides 491–B–5
HE 20.2109:	Focus 491–B–7
HE 20.2110:	Report HSRD-(series) 491–B–2
HE 20.2111:	HSRD Briefs (numbered) 491–B–3
HE 20.2112:	Reprint Series (numbered) 491–B–4
HE 20.2113:	Publications Reports (numbered) 491–B–6
HE 20.2114:	Conference Series 491–B–8

National Center for Health Statistics

HE 20.2201:	Annual Report 508–A–1
HE 20.2202:	General Publications 508
HE 20.2206:	Regulations, Rules, and Instructions 509
HE 20.2208:	Handbooks, Manuals, Guides 509
HE 20.2209:	Monthly Vital Statistics Report 508–B
HE 20.2210:	Vital and Health Statistics 500–E
HE 20.2211:	Annual Report of United States National Committee on Vital and Health Statistics, fiscal year 492–A (Rev. 1968)
HE 20.2212:	Vital Statistics of U.S. 510
HE 20.2213:	Bibliographies and Lists of Publications 508–G
HE 20.2214:	Proceedings of National Meeting of Public Health Conference on Records and Statistics (annual) 509–A
HE 20.2215:	Health Resources Statistics (annual) 509–B

Center for Disease Control

HE 20.2302:	General Publications 504
HE 20.2308:	Handbooks, Manuals, Guides 505–A
HE 20.2310:	Morbidity and Mortality Weekly Report 508–A
HE 20.2313:	Reported Tuberculosis Data (annual) 500–D

National Institute of Mental Health

HE 20.2402:	General Publications 507–B–5
HE 20.2408:	Handbooks, Manuals, Guides 507–B–10
HE 20.2408/2:	Social Seminar Discussion Guide Series 507–B–10
HE 20.2409:	Psychopharmacology Bulletin (quarterly) 507–Z–1
HE 20.2409/2:	Psychopharmacology Abstracts 507–Z
HE 20.2410:	Mental Health Digest (monthly) 507–T
HE 20.2412:	National Institute of Mental Health Support Programs 507–B–6 (Rev. 1969)
HE 20.2413:	Bulletin of Suicidology 507–B–4
HE 20.2413/2:	Bulletin of Suicidology, Supplements 507–B–4
HE 20.2414:	Schizophrenia Bulletin 507–B–7
HE 20.2415:	Mental Health Statistics Series 491–A
HE 20.2415/2:	Mental Health Statistics: Current Facility Reports 497–A
HE 20.2417:	Bibliographies and Lists of Publications 507–B–9
HE 20.2418:	Mental Health Directory 506–C
HE 20.2419:	Mental Health Program Reports 507–B–2
HE 20.2420:	Crime and Delinquency Abstracts 506–B
HE 20.2420/2:	Crime and Delinquency Issues, Monograph Series 507–B–13
HE 20.2420/3:	Crime and Delinquency Topics, Monograph Series 507–B–13
HE 20.2422:	Saint Elizabeths Hospital Publications 512
HE 20.2423:	Mental Health Research Grant Awards (fiscal year) 507–B–11
HE 20.2424:	Survey and Reports Section, Statistical Notes (numbered) 507–B–12
HE 20.2425:	Innovations, Mental Health Services, Progress Reports 507–B–14

Health Care Facilities Service

HE 20.2502:	General Publications 486–A–2
HE 20.2509:	Hill-Burton Project Register 486–C
HE 20.2509/2:	Hill-Burton Program Progress Report 486–C
HE 20.2511:	Health Facilities Series 486–D

Community Health Service

HE 20.2552:	General Publications 512–E–1
HE 20.2558:	Handbooks, Manuals, Guides 512–E–2

Regional Medical Programs Service

HE 20.2602:	General Publications 483–L–1
HE 20.2608:	Handbooks, Manuals, Guides 483–L–2
HE 20.2610:	Progress Report, Regional Medical Programs for Heart Disease, Cancer, Stroke, and Related Diseases 483–L
HE 20.2611:	Selected Bibliography of Regional Medical Programs 483–L–3
HE 20.2612:	Directory of On-Going Research in Smoking and Health 483–L–4

Indian Health Service

HE 20.2652:	General Publications 486–I–2
HE 20.2658:	Handbooks, Manuals, Guides 486–I–1
HE 20.2659:	Dental Services for American Indians and Alaskan Natives (annual) 486–F
HE 20.2661:	Indian Health Trends and Services (annual) 486–I–3

Federal Health Program Service

HE 20.2702:	General Publications 494–C–1
HE 20.2709:	Annual Statistical Summary, Fiscal Year 494–C
HE 20.2710:	Automated Multiphasic Health Testing Bibliography 494–C–2
HE 20.2710/2:	Bibliographies and Lists of Publications 494–C–3

Maternal and Child Health Service

HE 20.2751:	Annual Report 483–V–6
HE 20.2752:	General Publications 483–V–1
HE 20.2755:	Laws 483–V–5
HE 20.2758:	Handbooks, Manuals, Guides 483–V–3
HE 20.2759:	Bibliographies and Lists of Publications 483–V–2
HE 20.2760:	MCHS Statistical Series 483–V–4

National Institute for Occupational Safety and Health

HE 20.2809:	Toxic Substances, Annual List 494–D–1

Community Environmental Management Bureau

HE 20.2852:	General Publications 512–F
HE 20.2859:	Injury Control Research Laboratory: Research Report ICRL–RR (series) 483–0

National Center for Family Planning Services

HE 20.2909:	Family Planning Digest (bi-monthly) 494–E–1

National Institutes of Health

HE 20.3001:	Annual Report 506–G
HE 20.3002:	General Publications 507
HE 20.3006:	Regulations, Rules, and Instructions 507–A–21
HE 20.3008:	Handbooks, Manuals, Guides 507–H
HE 20.3009:	NIH Publications List 506–A
HE 20.3009/3:	Periodicals Currently Received in NIH Library 506–A
HE 20.3011:	Computer Research and Technology Division: Technical Reports 483–U
HE 20.3012:	Bibliographies and Lists of Publications 506–A
HE 20.3013:	Public Health Service Grants and Awards 507–D

HE 20.3013/2: Research Grants Index (annual) 507–D
HE 20.3013/2–2: NIH Research Grants 507–D
HE 20.3014: Resources for Biomedical Research and Education, Reports 507–U
HE 20.3015: Associated Training Programs in Medical and Biological Sciences, at National Institutes of Health (annual) 507–A–24
HE 20.3016: NIH Almanac (annual) 507–A–23
HE 20.3017: Scientific Directory and Annual Bibliography 506–A–5
HE 20.3018: NIH Public Advisory Groups: Authority, Structure, Functions 507–N
HE 20.3018/2: NIH Public Advisory Groups: Roster of Members 507–N
HE 20.3019: Addresses 507–A–17
HE 20.3021: Nursing Clinical Conference Presented by Nursing Department of Clinical Center, National Institutes of Health 507–A–19
HE 20.3022: DRG [Division of Research Grants] Newsletter) 506–E
HE 20.3023: Medical and Health Related Sciences Thesaurus 506–F
HE 20.3024: Progress Against Cancer 507–G

Health Manpower Education Bureau

HE 20.3102: General Publications 507–D–1
HE 20.3108: Handbooks, Manuals, Guides 507–D–3
HE 20.3109: Health Manpower Source Book 507–D–2
HE 20.3110: Nurses in Public Health 493–C
HE 20.3111: Current Research Project Grants (annual) 507–D–4
HE 20.3112: Fluoridation Census (annual) 483–G
HE 20.3113: Bibliographies and Lists of Publications 507–D–5
HE 20.3114: DMI [Division of Manpower Intelligence] Reports 507–D–6
HE 20.3114/2: Health Manpower Data Series 507–D–7
HE 20.3114/3: Health Manpower Clearinghouse Series 507–D–7

National Cancer Institute

HE 20.3152: General Publications 507–G–2
HE 20.3153/2: Information Bulletin (annual) 507–G–4
HE 20.3159: Carcinogenesis Abstracts (monthly) 507–A–1
HE 20.3160: Cancer Chemotherapy Reports, Pt. 1 507–A–9
HE 20.3160/2: Cancer Chemotherapy Reports, Pt. 2 507–A–9
HE 20.3160/3: Cancer Chemotherapy Reports, Pt. 3 507–A–9
HE 20.3161: Journal of National Cancer Institute 488
HE 20.3162: NCI Monographs 507–L
HE 20.3163: Progress Against Cancer, Report by National Advisory Cancer Council 507–G
HE 20.3164: Chemotherapy Fact Sheets 507–G–1
HE 20.3165: Bibliographies and Lists of Publications 507–G–3
HE 20.3166: NCI Research Reports (unnumbered) 507–V
HE 20.3167: Viral Tumorigenesis Report (semiannual) 507–G–5

National Heart and Lung Institute

HE 20.3202: General Publications 507–E–1
HE 20.3208: Handbooks, Manuals, Guides 507–E–2
HE 20.3209: Fibrinolysis, Thrombolysis, and Blood Clotting Bibliography 506–A–3
HE 20.3210: Medical Devices Application Program, Annual Report 507–E–3

National Institute of Allergy and Infectious Diseases

HE 20.3252: General Publications 505–A–1

National Institute of Arthritis and Metabolic Diseases

HE 20.3302: General Publications 507–A–25
HE 20.3308: Handbooks, Manuals, Guides 507–A–26
HE 20.3309: Endocrinology Index (bimonthly) 507–A–20
HE 20.3310/2: Diabetes Literature Index, Annual Index Issue 507–A–15

HE 20.3311: Artificial Kidney Bibliography (quarterly) 506–A–2
HE 20.3313: Gastroenterology Abstracts and Citations (monthly) 507–A–14
HE 20.3314: Annual Contractors Conference of Artificial Kidney Program Proceedings 506–A–6

National Institute of Child Health and Human Development

HE 20.3352: General Publications 506–D–2
HE 20.3361: Bibliographies and Lists of Publications 506–D–3
HE 20.3362: Population Research Reports (numbered) 506–A–4
HE 20.3362/2: Federal Program in Population Research Inventory of Population Research Supported by Federal Agencies During Fiscal Year 506–D–4
HE 20.3362/3: CPR Population Research (series) 506–D–5

National Institute of Dental Research

HE 20.3402: General Publications 507–O–1
HE 20.3408: Handbooks, Manuals, Guides 507–O–2
HE 20.3409: Dental Caries Research, Catalog of Dental Caries Research Project Sponsored During Fiscal Year by Federal and Non-Federal Organizations 507–O–3

National Institute of General Medical Sciences

HE 20.3451: Annual Report 497–B
HE 20.3452: General Publications 497–C–1

National Institute of Neurological Disease and Stroke

HE 20.3502: General Publications 507–L–2
HE 20.3510: NINDS Monographs 507–L–1
HE 20.3511: Parkinson's Disease and Related Disorders: Citations from the Literature 507–L–3
HE 20.3511/2: Parkinson's Disease and Related Disorders: International Directory of Scientists 507–L–5
HE 20.3511/3: Parkinson's Disease and Related Disorders: Cumulative Bibliography 527–L–3
HE 20.3512: NINDS Research Profiles (annual) 507–A–6
HE 20.3513: Bibliographies and Lists of Publications 507–L–4
HE 20.3513/2: Biblio-Profile of Human Communication & Its Disorders 507–L–4

National Institute of Environmental Health Sciences

HE 20.3552: General Publications 507–P–1

National Library of Medicine

HE 20.3601: Annual Report 508–L
HE 20.3602: General Publications 508–D
HE 20.3608: Handbooks, Manuals, Guides 508–K
HE 20.3608/2: Film Reference Guide for Medicine and Allied Sciences (annual) 508–H
HE 20.3608/4: National Medical Audiovisual Center Catalog 497–A
HE 20.3609: National Library of Medicine Current Catalog 508–J
HE 20.3609/2: National Library of Medicine Current Catalog, Cumulative Listing 508–J
HE 20.3609/3: National Library of Medicine Current Catalog, Annual Cumulation 508–J
HE 20.3610: Monthly Bibliography of Medical Reviews 508–F
HE 20.3610/2: Bibliography of Medical Reviews (cumulations) 508–F
HE 20.3612: Index Medicus, including Bibliography of Medical Reviews (monthly) 508–E
HE 20.3612/2: Abridged Index Medicus (monthly) 508–E–1
HE 20.3612/2–2: Cumulated Abridged Index Medicus, 508–E–1
HE 20.3612/3: Cumulated Index Medicus 508–E
HE 20.3613: Toxicity Bibliography (quarterly) 508–M
HE 20.3614: Bibliographies and Lists of Publications 508–F

471-404 O - 72 - 3

HE 20.3615:	Bibliography of the History of Medicine (annual, cumulated every five years) 508–F
HE 20.3616:	Selected References on Environmental Quality as It Relates to Health 508–H–2
HE 20.3617:	Current Bibliography of Epidemiology (monthly) 508–H–3

John E. Fogarty International Center for Advanced Study in the Health Sciences

HE 20.3701/2:	National Institutes of Health Annual Report of International Activities (fiscal year) 507–C–4
HE 20.3702:	General Publications 507–C–1
HE 20.3709:	Public Health Service International Postdoctoral Research Fellowships, Awards For Study In United States 507–C–2
HE 20.3710:	Fogarty International Center Proceedings 507–C–3

National Eye Institute

HE 20.3759:	Statistics on Blindness in Model Reporting Area (annual) 507–Y
HE 20.3759/2:	Conference of Model Reporting Area For Blindness Proceedings (annual) 507–Y

Food and Drug Administration

HE 20.4002:	General Publications 475
HE 20.4003/3:	FDA Drug Bulletin 475–Q
HE 20.4005:	Laws 475–B
HE 20.4006:	Regulations, Rules, & Instructions 478
HE 20.4008:	Handbooks, Manuals, Guides 475–G
HE 20.4009:	FDA Clinical Experience Abstracts (biweekly) 475–L
HE 20.4010:	FDA Papers 475–H
HE 20.4012:	National Drug Code Directory 475–N
HE 20.4013:	FDA Current Drug Information 474–A
HE 20.4015:	FDA Publications (numbered) 475–A
HE 20.4016:	Bibliographies and Lists of Publications 475–F
HE 20.4020:	Flammable Fabrics, Annual Report 475–O
HE 20.4022:	Public Advisory Committees: Authority, Structure, Functions, Members 475–P
HE 20.4023:	Selected Technical Publications (semi-annual) 475–R

Radiological Health Bureau

HE 20.4102:	General Publications 498–B–2
HE 20.4108:	Handbooks, Manuals, Guides 498–B–1
HE 20.4109:	BRH/NERHL (Northeastern Radiological Health Laboratory Series) 498–B–5
HE 20.4110:	BRH/DEP [Division of Electronic Products] (series) 468–A–5
HE 20.4111:	BRH/OBD (series) 498–B–4
HE 20.4112:	BRH/DMRE [Division of Medical Radiation Exposure] (series) 483–M
HE 20.4113:	BRH/ORO [Office of Regional Operations] Series 468–A–4
HE 20.4114:	BRH/DBE [Division of Biological Effects] (series) 468–A–6

Child Development Office

HE 21.2:	General Publications 454–C–1
HE 21.8:	Handbooks, Manuals, Guides 454–C–4
HE 21.8/2:	Child Development Office Manuals (numbered) 445–L
HE 21.9/2:	Children Today 449
HE 21.10:	Publications of Office of Child Development 454–C–2
HE 21.11:	Day Care USA [Publications] 454–C–3

Children's Bureau

HE 21.102:	General Publications 452
HE 21.108:	Handbooks, Manuals, Guides 452–C
HE 21.109:	Youth Reports 454–B
HE 21.110:	Publications (numbered) 453

HE 21.111:	Folders 451
HE 21.112:	Research Relating to Children Bulletin (numbered) 453–A
HE 21.113:	Bibliographies and Lists of Publications 450
HE 21.114:	Headliner Series 452–B

Head Start and Child Service Program Bureau

HE 21.202:	General Publications 445–N–2
HE 21.208:	Handbooks, Manuals, Guides 445–N–1
HE 21.208/2:	Healthy, That's Me, Parents Handbook 445–N–1
HE 21.210:	Caring for Children (series) 445–N–3
HE 21.211:	Bibliographies and Lists of Publications 445–N–4
HE 21.212:	Project Head Start Series 857–H–12

HOUSING AND URBAN DEVELOPMENT DEPARTMENT

HH 1.1:	Annual Report 581
HH 1.2:	General Publications 582
HH 1.5:	Laws 583
HH 1.6:	Regulations, Rules, & Instructions 584
HH 1.6/3:	Handbooks, Manuals, Guides 582–E
HH 1.6/6:	HUD Handbooks (numbered) 582–E
HH 1.6/7:	HUD Guides (numbered) 582–E
HH 1.7:	Addresses 581–C
HH 1.15/4:	HUD Newsletter 582–L
HH 1.23:	Bibliographies & Lists of Publications 581–D
HH 1.23/3:	Housing and Planning References, New Series 582–D
HH 1.26:	Urban Planning Assistance Program Project Directory 584–F
HH 1.32:	HUD International Country Reports 581–E–3
HH 1.35:	HUD Clearinghouse Service HCS–(series) 582–J
HH 1.36:	HUD Challenge (bimonthly) 582–K
HH 1.37:	Government National Mortgage Association: Annual Report 582–A–1
HH 1.38:	HUD Statistical Yearbook (annual) 582–M
HH 1.39:	Environmental Planning Papers 581–E
HH 1.40/2:	HUD International Briefs 581–E–1
HH 1.40/3:	HUD International Supplement 581–E–1
HH 1.40/4:	HUD International Information Sources Series 581–E–1
HH 1.41:	Biennial HUD Awards for Design Excellence (numbered) 581–E–2
HH 1.42:	Model Cities Management Series, Bulletins (numbered) 581–E–4
HH 1.46:	Community Development Evaluation Series 581–E–5

Federal Housing Administration

HH 2.2:	General Publications 589
HH 2.5:	Laws 592
HH 2.6:	Regulations, Rules, & Instructions 594
HH 2.6/6:	Handbooks, Manuals, Guides 589–A
HH 2.6/7:	Technical Standards Training Guide (series) 589–A
HH 2.7:	Land Planning Bulletin 591–A
HH 2.12:	Technical Circulars 593–A
HH 2.17:	Minimum Property Requirements for Properties of 1 or 2 Living Units 593
HH 2.17/3:	Minimum Property Requirements (miscellaneous) 593
HH 2.17/4:	Minimum Property Standards for 1 and 2 Living Units 593
HH 2.22:	Statement of Financial Condition (annual) 593–B
HH 2.28:	Analysis of [Various Areas] Housing Markets 593–E

Housing Assistance Administration

HH 3.	Reports & Publications 599

Land and Facilities Development Administration

HH 5.	Reports and Publications 586

471-404 O - 72 - 4

International Development Agency

S 18.1:	Report to Congress on the Foreign Assistance Program 900–C–3
S 18.2:	General Publications 900–C–2
S 18.6/2:	Procurement Regulations 900–C–5
S 18.8:	Handbooks, Manuals, Guides 900–C–4
S 18.15:	Addresses 900–C–1
S 18.28:	Proposed Foreign Aid Program 1056–D
S 18.33:	Development Digest 900–C–6

Peace Corps

S 19.	Reports and Publications 900–D

SMALL BUSINESS ADMINISTRATION

SBA 1.1:	Annual Report 901–A
SBA 1.2:	General Publications 901–B
SBA 1.3:	Small Business Bibliographies 901–K
SBA 1.6:	Regulations, Rules & Instructions 901–O
SBA 1.10/2:	Management Aids for Small Manufacturers Annuals 901–E
SBA 1.11:	Technical Aids for Small Manufacturers 901–I (Rev. 1969)
SBA 1.12:	Small Bus. Management Series 901–C
SBA 1.13/3:	U.S. Gov't Purchasing & Specifications Directory 901–D
SBA 1.14/2:	Small Marketers Aids Annuals 901–J
SBA 1.15:	Starting and Managing Series 901–L
SBA 1.17:	Addresses 901–T
SBA 1.18:	Small Business Administration Publications (lists) 901–N
SBA 1.18/2:	Bibliographies and Lists of Publications 901–N
SBA 1.18/3:	Classification of Management Publications 901–N
SBA 1.19:	Handbooks, Manuals, Guides 901–P
SBA 1.24:	Administrative Management Course Program Topics 901–S

SECURITIES AND EXCHANGE COMMISSION

SE 1.1:	Annual Report 903
SE 1.2:	General Publications 904
SE 1.5:	Laws 906
SE 1.6:	Regulations, Rules & Instructions 907
SE 1.9:	Official Summary of Security Transactions & Holdings Reported to S.E.C. 906–A
SE 1.11:	Decisions and Reports 908
SE 1.16:	Securities Traded on Exchanges under Securities Exchange Act 907–B
SE 1.19:	Judicial Decisions 905
SE 1.20:	Statistical Bulletin 908–A
SE 1.24:	Accounting Series Releases 902 (Rev. 1969).
SE 1.25/12:	Securities and Exchange Commission News Digest (daily) 908–B
SE 1.27:	Directory of Companies Filing Annual Reports under Securities Exchange Act 903–A

SMITHSONIAN INSTITUTION

SI 1.1:	Smithsonian Year 909
SI 1.1/2:	National Zoological Park, Annual Report 910–J
SI 1.2:	General Publications 910
SI 1.12:	Annals of Astrophysical Observatory 909–A
SI 1.12/2:	Smithsonian Contributions to Astrophysics 909–B
SI 1.17/2:	Bibliographies and Lists of Publications 909–C
SI 1.24:	Smithsonian Torch (monthly) 910–A
SI 1.25:	Atoll Research Bulletins (numbered) 910–C
SI 1.26:	Smithsonian Contributions to the Earth Sciences (numbered series) 910–B
SI 1.27:	Smithsonian Contribution to Zoology 910–D
SI 1.28:	Smithsonian Studies in History and Technology (numbered) 910–F
SI 1.29:	Smithsonian Contribution to Botany 910–E

SI 1.30:	Smithsonian Contribution to Paleobiology (numbered) 910–G
SI 1.31:	Addresses 909–A–1
SI 1.33:	Smithsonian Contributions to Anthropology 921–A
SI 1.34:	Archives and Special Collections of Smithsonian Institution (numbered) 910–H
SI 1.35:	Calendar of the Smithsonian Institution (monthly) 910–I

National Museum

SI 3.2:	General Publications 921
SI 3.3:	Bulletins 919
SI 3.8:	Contributions from National Herbarium 920
SI 3.9:	Bibliographies and Lists of Publications 918–A
SI 3.10:	Handbooks, Manuals, Guides 921

American Historical Association

SI 4.1:	Annual Report 915

National Collection of Fine Arts

SI 6.2:	General Publications 916

National Gallery of Art

SI 8.2:	General Publications 917
SI 8.9:	Report and Studies in the History of Art (annual) 917

National Air Museum

SI 9.9:	Smithsonian Annals of Flight 922–A

National Portrait Gallery

SI 11.2:	General Publications 922–B

TREASURY DEPARTMENT

T 1.1:	Annual Report on State of Finances 923
T 1.2:	General Publications 925
T 1.3:	Treasury Bulletin 926–A
T 1.4/2:	Department Circulars 924
T 1.4/3:	Department Circulars, Public Debt Series 924
T 1.5:	Daily Statement of U.S. Treasury 923–A–1
T 1.5/2:	Monthly Statement of Receipts & Expenditures of U.S. Government 923–A–2
T 1.10:	Regulations, Rules & Instructions 926
T 1.10/2:	Handbooks, Manuals, Guides 926
T 1.11/4:	Customs Bulletin (bound volumes) 927
T 1.44:	Tax Policy Research Studies 925–B
T 1.45:	Foreign Credits by the United States Government (semiannual) 925–C

Comptroller of Currency

T 12.1:	Annual Report 946
T 12.2:	General Publications 947

Customs Bureau

T 17.1:	Annual Reports 950–C
T 17.2:	General Publications 950
T 17.5/2:	Handbooks, Manuals, Guides 950–A
T 17.9:	Customs Regulations of U.S. 948
	——Revised Pages 948–A
T 17.9/2:	——Pt. 2, Measurement of Vessels 948
T 17.10:	Merchant Marine Statistics 951

Engraving & Printing Bureau

T 18.2:	General Publications 953

Internal Revenue Service

T 22.1:	Annual Report 955
T 22.2:	General Publications 956
T 22.17:	Regulations (numbered) 961
T 22.17/2:	Regulations, Alcohol Tax Unit 954
T 22.17/3:	Code of Federal Regulations, Title 26 961
T 22.17/4:	Code of Federal Regulations, Title 27 954
T 22.19:	Regulations, Rules & Instructions 961

TD 4.9: FAA Aviation News 431–A–11
 Summary of Airworthiness Directives:
TD 4.10/2: —Small Aircraft 431–A–15
TD 4.10/3: —Large Aircraft 431–A–15
TD 4.11: International Notams 431–A–9
TD 4.12: Airman's Information Manual 431–C–5
TD 4.13: Status of Federal Aviation Regulations 431–C–13
TD 4.14: Airport Activity Statistics of Certified Air Carriers (semiannual) 177–A
TD 4.15: Aircraft Type Certificate Data Sheets and Specifications 431–C–2
TD 4.15/2: Aircraft Engine and Propeller Type Certificate Data Sheets and Specifications 431–C–2
TD 4.17: FAA publications 431–A–1
TD 4.17/2: Selected Technical Reports, Information Retrieval Bulletin 431–A–1
TD 4.18: Census of U.S. Civil Aircraft 431–A–16
TD 4.18/2: United States Civil Aircraft Register 431–F–5
TD 4.19: FAA Air Traffic Activity 431–C–1
TD 4.19/2: Air Traffic Patterns for IFR and VFR Aviation 431–C–1
TD 4.19/3: Enroute IFR Air Traffic Survey, Peak Day, Fiscal Year 431–D–4
TD 4.19/4: Military Air Traffic Activity Report 431–C–1
TD 4.20: FAA Statistical Handbook of Aviation 431–C–14
TD 4.21: National Field Office Directory (triannual) 431–A–14
TD 4.24: Standard Specifications for Construction of Airports 431–C–15
TD 4.28: Acceptable Methods, Techniques, and Practices: Aircraft Alterations 431–F–6
TD 4.28/2: Acceptable Methods, Techniques, and Practices: Aircraft Inspection Repair 431–F–7
TD 4.33: National Aviation System Plan 431–A–17
TD 4.33/2: National Aviation System Policy Summary 431–A–17
TD 4.35: Commuter Air Carrier Operators 431–A–18
TD 4.36: Summary of Supplemental Type Certificates 431–A–5

Airports Service

TD 4.102: General Publications 982–E–1
TD 4.108: Handbooks, Manuals, Guides 431–H–2
TD 4.109: National Airport Plan 431–C–7
TD 4.110: Airports Service, Standards Division Index of Advisory Circulars 431–H–3
TD 4.111: Airport Design Standards 431–C–4

Aviation Medicine Office

TD 4.202: General Publications 431–E–3
TD 4.208: Handbooks, Manuals, Guides 431–E–2
TD 4.209: Aviation Medical Education Series 431–E–6
TD 4.210: Aviation Medical Reports, AM Series 431–E–4
TD 4.211: Directory, Aviation Medical Examiners 431–E–1

Air Traffic Service

TD 4.302: General Publications 431–D–5
TD 4.308: Handbooks, Manuals, Guides 431–D–1
TD 4.309: International Flight Information Manual 431–C–18
TD 4.310: Location Identifiers 431–D–3

Flight Standards Service

TD 4.402: General Publications 431–F–4
TD 4.408: Handbooks, Manuals, Guides 431–F–3
TD 4.409: General Aviation Inspection Aids, Summary and Supplements 431–C–6

Systems Research and Development Service

TD 4.502: General Publications 431–B–2 (rev.)

Coast Guard

TD 5.2: General Publications 934
TD 5.3: Bulletins (numbered) 931–A
TD 5.4/3: Boating Safety Circular 941–B
TD 5.5: Laws 935
TD 5.6: Regulations, Rules, & Instructions 943
TD 5.8: Handbooks, Manuals, Guides 934–A
TD 5.9: Light List:
 —Vol. 1, 2, Atlantic and Gulf Coast 936
 —Vol. 3 Pacific Coast 940
 —Vol. 4 Great Lakes 937
 —Vol. 5 Mississippi River System 939
TD 5.11: Boating Statistics 941–A
TD 5.12: Monthly Supplement to Merchant Vessels of the United States 950–B
TD 5.12/2: Merchant Vessels of U.S. 950
TD 5.13: Proceedings of Merchant Marine Council 941
TD 5.15: Coast Guard Academy Cadet Profile 982–F–1
TD 5.16: Coast Guard Academy Catalog 930–B
TD 5.18: Oceanographic Reports 940–B
TD 5.19: Register 942
TD 5.19/2: Register of C. G. Reserve 942
TD 5.20: Equipment Lists 933–A
TD 5.23: Proceedings of National Data Buoy Systems Scientific Advisory Meeting 935–A
TD 5.24: On Scene, the National Maritime SAR Review 931–C

Saint Lawrence Seaway Development Corporation

TD 6.1: Annual Report 1074–C

Urban Mass Transportation Administration

TD 7.9: Directory of Research Development and Demonstration Projects 982–H

National Highway Traffic Safety Administration

TD 8.2: General Publications 982–D–1
TD 8.6: Regulations, Rules and Instructions 982–D–3
TD 8.8: Handbooks, Manuals, Guides 982–D–3
TD 8.8/2: Community Action Program for Traffic Safety, Guides (numbered) 982–D–8
TD 8.9: Motor Vehicle Safety Defect Recall Campaigns Reported to National Highway Traffic Safety Administration by Domestic and Foreign Vehicle Manufacturers (quarterly) 982–D–2
TD 8.10: Highway Safety Literature, Announcement of Recent Acquisitions (weekly) 982–D–4
TD 8.10/2: Highway Safety Literature Index 982–D–4
TD 8.10/3: Highway Safety Literature Annual Cumulations 982–D–4
TD 8.11/2: Multidisciplinary Accident Investigation Summaries 982–D–10
TD 8.12: Report on Activities under National Traffic and Motor Vehicle Safety Act 982–D–7
TD 8.12/2: Report on Activities under Highway Safety Act 982–D–7
TD 8.12/3: Report on Activities of National Highway Traffic Safety Administration and Federal Highway Administration under Highway Safety Act and National Traffic and Motor Vehicle Safety Act 982–D–7
TD 8.14: Consumer Information Series 982–D–6
TD 8.14/2: Consumer Aid Series (numbered) 982–D–9

VETERANS ADMINISTRATION

VA 1.1: Annual Report 983
VA 1.2: General Publications 985
VA 1.6: Regulations, Rules & Instructions 989
VA 1.10: Handbooks, Manuals, Guides (unnumbered) 987
VA 1.10/3: Program Guide PG series 987
VA 1.10/4: Guides, G (series) 987
VA 1.10/5: Handbooks (numbered) 987
VA 1.18: Manuals 987

VA 1.19:	Pamphlets 988
VA 1.20:	Index to V.A. Publications 986
VA 1.20/2:	Bibliographies & Lists of Publications 983–A
VA 1.20/3:	Bibliographies (numbered) 983–A
VA 1.22:	Information Bulletins 986–A
VA 1.23/2:	Medical Bulletin 987–A
VA 1.23/3:	Bulletin of Prosthetics Research, BPR 983–B
VA 1.34:	VA Fact Sheets IS-(series) 989–B
VA 1.38:	Training Guides 989–A
VA 1.40/2:	Transactions of Research Conference on Pulmonary Diseases 988–A
VA 1.42:	Proceedings of Annual Clinical Spinal Cord Injury Conference 989–C
VA 1.43:	Medical Research in Veterans Administration (annual) 987–B
VA 1.43/2:	VA Medical Research Conference Abstracts 987–B
VA 1.43/3:	Highlights of VA Medical Research 987–B
VA 1.43/4:	Medical Research Program 987–B
VA 1.44:	VA Benefits in Brief 989–D
VA 1.45:	Technical Reports 989–E
VA 1.46:	Government Life Insurance Programs for Veterans & Servicemen 985–A
VA 1.47:	Search, Administrative Research Bulletin 988–B
VA 1.48:	VA Monographs (numbered) 989–F
VA 1.48/2:	Research Monographs (numbered) 989–F

CONGRESS

	Congressional Record:
X	—(bound) 993
X/a	—(daily) 994
XJH	House Journal 1030
XJS	Senate Journal 1047

House of Representatives

Y 1.2:	General Publications 998
Y 1.2/2:	Calendar of United States House of Representatives and History of Legislation 998–A

Senate

Y 1.3:	General Publications 998
Y 1.3/3:	Calendar of Business, Senate 998–B

COMMISSIONS, COMMITTEES, AND BOARDS

Y 3.	Reports and Publications 1089

ADMINISTRATIVE CONFERENCE OF UNITED STATES

Y 3.Ad6:1	Annual Report 1049–G
Y 3.Ad6:9	Recommendations and Reports of Administrative Conference of United States 1049–H

ADVISORY COMMISSION ON INFORMATION

Y 3.Ad9/7:	Reports and Publications 1049–B

ADVISORY COMMISSION ON INTERGOVERNMENTAL RELATIONS

Y 3.Ad9/8:	Reports and Publications 1049–D

ADVISORY COMMISSION ON INTERNATIONAL EDUCATION AND CULTURAL AFFAIRS

Y 3.Ad9/9:	Reports and Publications 1049–F

FEDERAL FIELD COMMITTEE FOR DEVELOPMENT PLANNING IN ALASKA

Y 3.Al 1s/4:	Reports and Publications 1063–A–1

AMERICAN BATTLE MONUMENTS COMMISSION

Y 3.Am3:	Publications 1050

APPALACHIAN REGIONAL COMMISSION

Y 3.Ap4/2:	Reports and Publications 1050–A

ATOMIC ENERGY COMMISSION

Y 3.At7:1	Annual Report to Congress 1053
Y 3.At7:2	General Publications 1051
Y 3.At7:3	Safety & Fire Protection Technical Bulletins 1052–A
Y 3.At7:5	Laws 1051–D
Y 3.At7:6	Regulations, Rules & Instructions (Miscellaneous) 1052
Y 3.At7:6–2	Rules and Regulations (title 10, chap. 1, CFR) 1052
Y 3.At7:6–3	Handbooks, Manuals, Guides 1051–F
Y 3.At7:6–4	AEC Licensing Guides 1051–F
Y 3.At7:16	Nuclear Science Abstracts 1051–A
Y 3.At7:16–4	Nuclear Data Tables 1051–A
Y 3.At7:16–5	Nuclear Science Abstracts Indexes 1051–A
Y 3.At7:22	Research & Development Reports 1051–C
Y 3.At7:34	Addresses 1051–N
Y 3.At7:36	Reactor Technology 1051–E
Y 3.At7:36	Reactor and Fuel Processing Technology (quarterly) 1051–E
Y 3.At7:37	Reactor and Fuel Processing Technology 1051–E
Y 3.At7:38	Reactor Materials (quarterly) 1051–E
Y 3.At7:39	Financial Report (annual) 1051–M
Y 3.At7:42	Trilinear Chart of Nuclides 1051
Y 3.At7:45	Nuclear Safety (quarterly) 1051–H
Y 3.At7:48	Fundamental Nuclear Energy Research (annual) 1051–I
Y 3.At7:49	Atomic Energy Commission Reports (Opinions & Decisions) (bound volumes) 1051–J
Y 3.At7:52	Isotopes & Radiation Technology (quarterly) 1051–L
Y 3.At7:56	Nuclear Industry (annual) 1051–O
Y 3.At7:58	Public Safety Newsletter 1051–P

FEDERAL INTERAGENCY COMMITTEE ON EDUCATION

Y 3.Ed 8:	Reports and Publications 1062–A

NATIONAL ADVISORY COUNCIL ON EDUCATION PROFESSIONS DEVELOPMENT

Y 3.Ed8/3:1	Annual Report 1091

EQUAL EMPLOYMENT OPPORTUNITY COMMISSION

Y 3.Eq2:	Reports and Publications 1059–A–1

EXPORT-IMPORT BANK OF UNITED STATES

Y 3.Ex7/3:1	Semi-annual Report 1061
Y 3.Ex7/3:2	General Publications 1060
Y 3.Ex7/3:5	Laws 1060
Y 3.Ex7/3:6	Regulations, Rules and Instructions 1060
Y 3.Ex7/3:9	Addresses 1060

FEDERAL COUNCIL FOR SCIENCE & TECHNOLOGY

Y 3.F31/16:	Reports and Publications 1061–B

FEDERAL RADIATION COUNCIL

Y 3.F31/17:	Reports and Publications 1063–E

FEDERAL COMMITTEE ON PEST CONTROL

Y 3.F31/18:	Reports and Publications 1061–C

FEDERAL COMMITTEE ON RESEARCH NATURAL AREAS

Y 3.F31/19:	Reports and Publications 1061–D

FEDERAL EXECUTIVE BOARD

Y 3.F31/20:	Reports and Publications 1061–E

FOREIGN CLAIMS SETTLEMENT COMMISSION

Y 3.F76/3:	Reports and Publications 1063–C

FOREIGN SCHOLARSHIPS BOARD

Y 3.F76/4:	Reports and Publications 1063–F

GREAT LAKES BASIN COMMISSION

Y 3.G79/3:	Reports and Publications 1063–G

ADVISORY COUNCIL ON HISTORIC PRESERVATION

Y 3.H62: Reports and Publications 1064–A

OLIVER WENDELL HOLMES DEVISE PERMANENT COMMITTEE

Y 3.H73: Reports and Publications 1063–D

INDIAN CLAIMS COMMISSION

Y 3.In2/6: Reports and Publications 1067

NATIONAL INDUSTRIAL POLLUTION CONTROL COUNCIL

Y 3.In2/8: Reports and Publications 1070–B–2

INTERDEPARTMENTAL COMMITTEE ON CHILDREN & YOUTH

Y 3.In8/6: Reports and Publications 1067–B

INTERDEPARTMENTAL COMMITTEE ON STATUS OF WOMEN

Y 3.In8/21: Reports and Publications 1067–I

INTER-AGENCY COMMITTEE ON MEXICAN–AMERICAN AFFAIRS

Y 3.In8/23: Reports and Publications 1067–K

LEWIS AND CLARK TRAIL COMMISSION

Y 3.L58: Reports and Publications 1067–J

MISSOURI BASIN INTER-AGENCY COMMITTEE

Y 3.M69: Reports and Publications 607

NATIONAL CAPITAL TRANSPORTATION AGENCY

Y 3.N21/21: Reports and Publications 1070–E

NATIONAL COMMISSION ON FOOD MARKETING

Y 3.N21/22: Reports and Publications 1070–G

FRANKLIN DELANO ROOSEVELT MEMORIAL COMMISSION

Y 3.R67: Reports and Publications 1073–A

SELECTIVE SERVICE SYSTEM

Y 3.Se4:1 Report of Director 1076
Y 3.Se4:2 General Publications 1075
Y 3.Se4:7 Selective Service Regulations (packets) 1077
Y 3.Se4:10–2 Handbooks, Manuals, Guides 1075
Y 3.Se4:13–2 Transmittal Memo. for Local Board Memo. 1079
Y 3.Se4:17 Special Monographs 1078
Y 3.Se4:20 Selective Service 1077–A
Y 3.Se4:22 Selective Service College Qualification Test, Bulletin of Information 1077–B

CABINET COMMITTEE ON OPPORTUNITIES FOR SPANISH SPEAKING PEOPLE

Y 3.Sp2/7: Reports and Publications 1067–K

SUBVERSIVE ACTIVITIES CONTROL BOARD

Y 3.Su1: Reports and Publications 1079–A

NATIONAL COMMISSION ON TECHNOLOGY, AUTOMATION, AND ECONOMIC PROGRESS

Y 3.T22: Reports and Publications 1070–F

TENNESSEE VALLEY AUTHORITY

Y 3.T25:1 Annual Report 1080
Y 3.T25:2 General Publications 1082
Y 3.T25:17 Technical Reports 1083

NATIONAL ADVISORY COUNCIL ON VOCATIONAL EDUCATION

Y 3.V85: Reports and Publications 1070–B–1

WATER RESOURCES COUNCIL

Y 3.W29: Reports and Publications 1090

WHITE HOUSE CONFERENCES

Y 3.W58/ Reports and Publications 1088

CONGRESS

NOTE.—Where only the name of the committee is given, the series represented are hearings of the particular committee.

Y 4.	Select and Special Committees (as appointed) 1009
Y 4.Ae8:	Comm. on Aeronautical and Space Sciences (Senate) 1032–A
Y 4.Ag8/1:	Comm. on Agriculture (House) 1010
Y 4.Ag8/2:	Comm. on Agriculture & Forestry (Senate) 1032
Y 4.Ap6/1:	Comm. on Appropriations (House) 1011
Y 4.Ap6/2:	Comm. on Appropriations (Senate) 1033
Y 4.Ar5/2:	Comm. on Armed Services (House) 1012
Y 4.Ar5/2a:	——Papers (numbered) 1012
Y 4.Ar5/3:	Comm. on Armed Services (Senate) 1034
Y 4.At7/2:	Joint Comm. on Atomic Energy 999
Y 4.B22/1:	Comm. on Banking & Currency (House) 1013
Y 4.B22/3:	Banking, Housing, and Urban Affairs Comm. on (Senate) 1035
Y 4.C73/2:	Committee on Commerce (Senate) 1041
Y 4.C76/7:	Joint Committee on Congressional Operations 1000–A
Y 4.D36:	Joint Comm. on Defense Production 999–A
Y 4.D63/1:	Comm. on District of Columbia (House) 1014
Y 4.D63/2:	Comm. on District of Columbia (Senate) 1036
Y 4.Ec7:	Economic Joint Committee 1000
Y 4.Ec7:Ec7	——Economic Indicators 997
Y 4.Ed8/1:	Comm. on Education & Labor (House) 1015
Y 4.F49:	Comm. on Finance (Senate) 1038
Y 4.F76/1:	Comm. on Foreign Affairs (House) 1017
Y 4.F76/2:	Comm. on Foreign Relations (Senate) 1039
Y 4.G74/6:	Committee on Government Operations (Senate) 1037
Y 4.G74/7:	Committee on Government Operations (House) 1016
Y 4.H81/3:	Comm. on House Administration (House) 1018
Y 4.In8/4:	Comm. on Interstate & Foreign Commerce (House) 1019
Y 4.In8/11:	Joint Comm. on Internal Revenue Taxation 1002
Y 4.In8/13:	Comm. on Interior & Insular Affairs (Senate) 1040
Y 4.In8/14:	Comm. on Interior & Insular Affairs (House) 1023
Y 4.In8/15:	Comm. on Internal Security (House) 1026
Y 4.J89/1:	Comm. on Judiciary (House) 1024
Y 4.J89/1:D63/24/	——District of Columbia Code & Supplements 990
Y 4.J89/1:Un3/3/	——United States Code & Supplements 991
Y 4.J89/2:	Comm. on Judiciary (Senate) 1042
Y 4.L11/2:	Comm. on Labor & Public Welfare (Senate) 1043
Y 4.L61/2:	Joint Committee on the Library 1003
Y 4.M53:	Comm. on Merchant Marine & Fisheries (House) 1021
Y 4.N22/4:	Joint Committee on Navajo-Hopi Indian Admin. 1021–A
Y 4.P84/10:	Comm. on Post Office & Civil Service (House) 1022
Y 4.P84/10:M31/5/	——Improved Manpower Management in Federal Government (semiannual) 1022–A

Y 4.P84/11:	Committee on Post Office and Civil Service (Senate) 1044	**Y 4.Sci 2:**	Comm. on Science and Astronautics (House) 1025–A
Y 4.P93/1:	Joint Committee on Printing 1004	**Y 4.Sm 1:**	Small Business Select Comm. (House) 1031
Y 4.P93/1:1	——Congressional Directory 992		
Y 4.P93/1:7	——Government Paper Specification Standards 1004–B	**Y 4.Sm 1/2:**	Small Business Select Comm. (Senate) 1049
Y 4.P96/10:	Comm. on Public Works (Senate) 1045	**Y 4.St2/3:**	Committee on Standards of Official Conduct (House) 1025–B
Y 4.P96/11:	Comm. on Public Works (House) 1024		
Y 4.R86/1:	Comm. on Rules (House) 1025	**Y 4.V64/3:**	Comm. on Veterans' Affairs (House) 1027
Y 4.R86/2:	Comm. on Rules & Administration (Senate) 1046	**Y 4.V64/4:**	Veterans Affairs Committee (Senate) 1046
		Y 4.W36:	Comm. on Ways & Means (House) 1028
		Y 7.1:	Memorial Addresses 1005

NOTE.—The following series (with the exception of Laws and Journals) are not classified but instead are designated by Congress, session and individual number (for example, House Document 23 of the 82d Congress, 1st Session would be 82–1:H.doc.23, Senate Document 23 would be 82–1:S.doc.23, House Bill 69 would be 82–1:H.R. 69, Senate Bill 52 would be 82–1:S.52, Senate Report 15 would be 82–1:S.rp.15 and House Report 26 would be 82–1:H rp.26) forming classes in themselves. The bound volumes of documents and reports may comprise more than one individual number, and are designated as being volumes of reports and documents of the particular Congress and session.

BILLS

Public Bills and Resolutions (House and Senate) 1006

DOCUMENTS

Bound Volumes (House and Senate):
—American Legion, Proceedings of National Convention 995–I
—Appropriations, Budget Estimates, etc. (financial statements) 995–E
—Boy Scouts of America and Girl Scouts of U.S.A., Annual Reports 995–P
—Daughters of American Revolution, Annual Report of National Society 995–B
—Disabled American Veterans, National Report 995–J
—House Manual (Rules and Manual of House of Representatives) 1029
—Miscellaneous Documents (bound) 995–G
—Proceedings of National Convention of Veterans of World War I of U.S. 995–Q
—Secretary of Senate, Report 995–M
—Senate Manual 1048
—United Spanish War Veterans, Proceedings of National Encampment 995–K
—Veterans of Foreign Wars of U.S., Proceedings of National Convention 995–L
Unbound (House and Senate documents) 996

JOURNALS

House Journal 1030   Classified as XJH: (Cong.-Session)
Senate Journal 1047   Classified as XJS: (Cong.-Session)

LAWS

Public Laws 575   Classified as GS–4.110: (Cong. & Nos.)

REPORTS

Bound Volumes
—Reports on **Public** Bills 1007–A
—Reports on **Private** Bills 1007–B
Unbound
—Reports on **Public** Bills, 1008–A
—Reports on **Private** Bills 1008–B

Work Sheet

Additions and changes to LIST OF CLASSES

Appendix II

Principles of the Superintendent of Documents Classification Scheme

Principles of the System[1]

The basis of the classification is the grouping together of the publications of any Government author—the various departments, bureaus, and agencies being considered the authors. In the grouping, the organizational structure of the United States Government is followed, that is, subordinate bureaus and divisions are grouped with the parent organization.

Author Symbols

Each executive department and agency, the Judiciary, Congress, and other major independent establishments are assigned a place in the scheme. The place is determined by the alphabetical designation assigned to each, as "A" for Agriculture Department, "Ju" for Judiciary, and "NS" for National Science Foundation, the designation usually being based on the name of the organization.

Subordinate Offices

To set off the subordinate bureaus and offices, numbers are added to the symbols with figure "1" being used for the parent organization and the secretary's or administrator's office. Beginning with the figure "2" the numbers are applied in numerical order to the subordinate bureaus and offices, these having been arranged alphabetically when the system was established, and new subordinate bureaus or offices having been given the next highest number. A period follows the combination of letters and numbers representing the bureau or office. For example:

Agriculture Department (including Secretary's Office)   A 1.
Forest Service   A 13.
Information Office   A 21.
Rural Electrification Administration   A 68.

Series Designations

The second breakdown in the scheme is for the various series of publications issued by a particular bureau or office. A number is assigned to each series and this number is followed by a colon.

In the beginning the following numbers were assigned for the types of publications common to most Government offices:

1: Annual reports
2: General publications (unnumbered publications of a miscellaneous nature)
3: Bulletins
4: Circulars

In setting up classes for new agencies or bureaus, these numbers were reserved for those types of publications. Later, new types common to most offices evolved and the following additional numbers were set aside in the classes of new agencies for particular types of series:

5: Laws (administered by the agency and published by it)
6: Regulations, rules, and instructions
7: Releases
8: Handbooks, manuals, guides

Any additional series issued by an office are given the next highest numbers in order of issuance—that is, as an office begins publication of a series the next highest number not already assigned to a series is assigned to the new series of the particular office.

Related Series

New series which are closely related to already existing series are now tied-in to the existing series so as to file side by side on the shelf. Originally no provision was made for this except in the case of separates from publications in a series. Tie-in is provided by use of the shilling mark after the number assigned to the existing series, followed by a digit for each related series starting with ''2''. (The ''1'' is not generally used in this connection since the existing series is the first.) Separates are distinguished by use of a lower case letter beginning with "a" rather than by numbers.

A theoretical example of these "tie-in" classes is as follows:

4: Circulars

4/a: Separates from Circulars (numbered)

4/b: Separates from Circulars (unnumbered)

4/2: Administrative Circulars

4/3: Technical Circulars

Class Stem

Thus by combining the designations for authors and those for the series published by the authors, we obtain the class stems for the various series of publications issued by the United States Government. For example:

A 1.10: Agriculture Yearbook

A 13.1: Annual Report of Chief of Forest Service

A 57.38: Soil Survey Reports

Book Numbers

The individual book number follows the colon. For numbered series the original edition of a publication gets simply the number of the book. For example, Department of Agriculture Leaflet 381 would be A 1.35:381. For revisions of numbered publications, the shilling mark and additional figures beginning the 2 are added, as: A 1.35:381/2, A 1.35:381/3, etc.

In the case of annuals, the last three digits of the year are used for the book number, e.g., Annual Report of Secretary of Agriculture, A 1.1:954. For reports or publications covering more than one year, a combination of the dates is used, e.g., Annual Register of the U.S. Naval Academy, 1954-1955 is D 208.107:954-55.

Unnumbered publications (other than continuations) are given a book number based on the principal subject word of the title, using a 2-figure Cutter table. An example is *Radioactive Heating of Vehicles Entering the Earth's Atmosphere*, NAS 1.2:R 11, "Radioactive" being the key subject word and the Cutter designation being R 11. Another publication, *Measurements of Radiation from Flow Fields of Bodies Flying Speeds up to 13.4 Kilometers per Second*, issued by the same agency, falling in the same series class (NAS 1.2:), and having the same Cutter number for the principal subject word, is individualized by adding the shilling mark and the figure 2, as NAS

1.2:R 11/2. Subsequent different publications in the same subject group which take the same Cutter designation would be identified as R 11/3, R 11/4, etc.

In assigning book numbers to unnumbered separates or reprints from whole publications, the 3-figure Cutter table is used. This is done for the purpose of providing for finer distinctions in class between publications whose principal subject words begin with the same syllable. The 3-figure table is also sometimes used in regular unnumbered series for the same purpose.

Another use of the 3-figure Cutter table is for non-Government publications which although not officially authored by a particular Government bureau or agency, may have been written by some of its personnel, or may be about it and its work, and it is desirable to have them filed on the shelf with the organization's own publications. The book numbers assigned to the non-Government publications are treated as decimals so as to file with the same subject groups but yet not disturb the sequence of book numbers of publications actually authored by the organization.

Revisions of unnumbered publications are identified by addition of the shilling mark and the last three digits of the year of revision. For example, if the first publication mentioned in the preceding paragraph was revised in 1964, the complete classification would read NAS 1.2:R 11/964. Subsequent revisions in the same year would be identified as 964-2, 964-3, etc.

Periodicals and other continuations are identified by number, or volume and number as the case may be. Volume and number are separated by use of the shilling mark. Some examples are:

Current Export Bulletin, No. 732, C 42.11/2:732

Marketing Information Guide, Vol. 17, No. 1, C 41.11:17/1

Unnumbered periodicals and continuations are identified by the year of issuance and order of issuance throughout the year. The last three digits of the year are used, and a number corresponding to the order of issuance within the year is added, the two being separated by the shilling mark. An example is:

United States Savings Bonds Issued and Redeemed, January 31, 1954, T 63.7:954/1

---

1. Excerpted from *An Explanation of the Superintendent of Documents Classification System.* Washington, D.C.: Library, Division of Public Documents, United States Government Printing Office, 1963, Revised 1970.

Appendix III

Agency Index to Superintendent of Documents Classification Scheme[1]

Health, Education, and Welfare Department	HE
Housing and Urban Development Department	HH
(Formerly Housing and Home Finance Agency)	
Interior Department	I
United States Information Agency	IA
Interstate Commerce Commission	IC
Justice Department	J
Judiciary (Courts of the United States)	Ju
Labor Department	L
Library of Congress	LC
National Labor Relations Board	LR
National Academy of Sciences	NA
National Aeronautics and Space Administration	NAS
National Capital Planning Commission	NC
National Credit Union Administration	NCU
National Foundation on the Arts and the Humanities	NF
National Mediation Board	NMB
National Science Foundation	NS
Post Office Department [U.S. Postal Service]	P
President of United States	Pr
Executive Office of the President	PrEx
National Railroad Adjustment Board	RA
Renegotiation Board	RnB
Railroad Retirement Board	RR
State Department	S
Small Business Administration	SBA
Securities and Exchange Commission	SE
Smithsonian Institution	SI
Treasury Department	T
Tariff Commission	TC
Transportation Department	TD
Veterans Administration	VA
Congress	X and Y

1. Excerpted from *An Explanation of the Superintendent of Documents Classification System*. Washington, D.C.: Library, Division of Public Documents, United States Government Printing Office, 1963, Revised 1970.

Appendix IV

Designated Depository Libraries: Library Practice[1]

Authorization: The law now in force provides a class of libraries in the United States in which certain Government publications are deposited for the use of the public. These libraries are known in the office of the Superintendent of Documents, Government Printing Office, where the distribution is made, as designated depository libraries. . . .

Discontinuance: Once a library has been designated a depository it cannot be removed from the list and another library designated in its place upon the election of a new Member of Congress. It remains a depository until it ceases to exist or vacates the privilege at its own request. . . . It can, however, be removed by the Superintendent of Documents for failure to abide by the laws governing the depository program. . . .

Regional Depositories: The 1962 amendments to the law provided for the designation of not more than two libraries in each State and the Commonwealth of Puerto Rico to be regional depositories. Such designations may be made by the Senators from the States and the Resident Commissioner in the case of Puerto Rico.

Libraries designated to be regional depositories must already be designated depositories.

Designation as a regional depository requires prior approval of the head of the library authority of the State or the Commonwealth of Puerto Rico.

In addition to fulfilling the requirements for regular depositories, they must receive and retain at least one copy of all Government publications made available to depositories, either in printed or microfacsimile form (except those authorized to be discarded by the Superintendent of Documents).

Within the region they serve, the regional depositories must provide interlibrary loan, reference service, and assistance for regular depository libraries in the disposal of unwanted Government publications as provided by law. They have the authority to permit regular depository libraries within the areas served by them to dispose of Government publications which they have retained for at least 5 years after first offering them to other depository libraries within their area, then to other libraries, and then if not wanted to discard.

Books Furnished: Depository libraries are permitted to receive one copy of all publications of the U.S. Government, except those determined by their issuing components to be required for official use only or those required for strictly administrative or operational purposes which have no public interest or educational value, and publications classified for reasons of national security. In addition to the exceptions noted, the so-called cooperative publications, which must necessarily be sold in order to be self-sustaining, are also excluded. These are primarily certain publications of the Library of Congress and those of the Clearinghouse for Federal Scientific and Technical Information.

Selective Plan: In view of the repeated requests from librarians of the designated depository libraries to be granted the privilege of selecting those public documents of the United States most suitable for their libraries, and which they would prefer to receive, instead of being compelled as formerly to receive the whole output of the Government Printing Office, all libraries are now on a selective basis. A classified list of the series and groups of Government Publications available for selection has been furnished to all depositories for their use in making selections. This list which is revised from time to time is furnished in card form with one card for each series or group of publications giving the distribution item number, the issuing agency, the series or group title, and brief descriptions where needed.

As new series are begun by existing Government agencies, or new agencies are established, additional cards for the list are furnished to depositories for them to select the new material if desired. Cards are furnished in duplicate and selections are made by return to the

Superintendent of Documents of one card for each series or group selected, properly marked with the depository's assigned library number. . . .

The annual appropriation act for the Government Printing Office, beginning with July 1, 1922, provides that no part of the sum appropriated shall be used to supply the depository libraries with any publications not requested by such libraries, and that request must be made in advance of printing. There is therefore no retroactive distribution of depository publications as only sufficient copies are printed to provide distribution to those libraries which have selected the series or group in which a particular publication falls, prior to time of printing.

Disposal of Books: The law requires that the Government publications, when forwarded to a depository, shall be made available for the free use of the general public, and must be retained permanently by all depository libraries not served by a regional depository, and by regional depositories themselves in either printed or microfacsimile form. The exceptions allowed by the present law are superseded publications and those issued later in bound form, which may be discarded as authorized by the Superintendent of Documents.

Depository libraries which are served by regional depositories may dispose of publications which they have retained for at least 5 years with the permission of and in accordance with instructions from the regional depository which serves their area.

Depository libraries within executive departments and independent agencies of the Federal Government are authorized to dispose of unwanted Government publications after first offering them to the Library of Congress and the National Archives.

1. Excerpted from *Government Depository Libraries, present laws governing designated depository libraries, Revised Apr. 1971.* 1971. (Joint Committee print, 92nd Congress, 1st session).

Appendix V

Designated Depository Libraries: History of Early Legislation[1]

Before the establishment of designated depositories, or any systematic methods for the distribution of public documents, special acts were passed at various times providing for the printing of a sufficient number of copies of the public journals of the Senate and House of Representatives for distribution to the executives of the several States and each branch of the State and territorial legislatures. Provision was also made at times for supplying these journals, the acts, and sometimes the documents and reports, to each university and college incorporated in each State, as well as to the incorporated historical societies throughout the country.

During the 13th Congress, second session, December 27, 1813, a resolution was adopted embodying these provisions which had heretofore been covered by special legislation, and not only directing distribution for a Congress, but "for every future Congress." Two hundred copies in addition to the usual number was the limit named for documents, and this, of course, was more than sufficient for the needs at that early day.

By joint resolutions approved July 20, 1840, and April 30, 1844, the number of copies of journals and documents printed was increased to 800.

A resolution of January 28, 1857, as amended by a resolution of

March 20, 1858, was the real basis of the institution of depositories. By these provisions the journals and documents which up to that time, were deposited in the Library of Congress for distribution by the Librarian, and 250 copies of those delivered to the Department of State for distribution by that Department to colleges and other literary institutions, were transferred to the jurisdiction of the Secretary of the Interior "for distribution to such colleges, public libraries, atheneums, literary and scientific institutions, and boards of trade or public associations as may be designated to him by the Representative in Congress from each congressional district and by the Delegate from each Territory in the United States.''

The following February, at the second session, 35th Congress (Feb. 5, 1859), an act was passed providing for "keeping and distributing all public documents" (11 Stat. 379). This act charged the Secretary of the Interior with "receiving, arranging, safekeeping, and distribution" of public documents "of every nature," already or hereafter directed by law to be printed or purchased for the use of the Government, "except such as are for the special use of Congress or the executive departments." It also empowered him to remove from the Congressional Library and other places all accumulations of books, journals, etc., and appropriated $22,000 for the purpose. He was directed by the act to keep accurate statistics of the receipt and distribution of all books.

Section 5 of this act further amended the resolution of January 28, 1857, by providing for the designation of a library by each of the Senators, and directing that the distribution should be made first to such States as had not yet been covered by distribution, and that in the future the distribution should be kept equal in each congressional district and territory.

All books, maps, charts, etc., heretofore deposited in the Department of State were also turned over to the Secretary of the Interior.

The act of February 5, 1859, was in force without amendment until March 2, 1861, at the 36th Congress, second session, when a long act to amend was passed (12 Stat. 244), the most important feature of which as affecting general distribution was contained in the first section, which gave the Secretary of the Interior the right to designate libraries to receive publications of which the edition was not sufficient to supply the regular depositories to be named by the Senators and Representatives. His power of selection was limited however, by a proviso in section 2, which stated that in the future the public documents to be distributed by the Secretary of the Interior should be sent to the institutions already designated, unless he should be satisfied that any such institution was no longer a suitable depository for the same. This act also contained a clause repealing all acts or parts of acts inconsistent with its provisions.

Upon the basis of these acts the Revised Statutes were compiled, and chapter 7, sections 497 to 511, pages 82 to 85, contain all operative provisions reenacted at that time and superseding all former enactments.

No legislation can be found prior to that contained in the General Printing Act of January 12, 1895, affecting the State and territorial libraries, and it is thought that it became customary to send documents regularly to these libraries, under the discretionary powers vested in the Secretary of the Interior which would account for their appearance on the depository list many years prior to 1895.

Designated Depository Libraries: Laws in Force[2]

1901. Definition of Government publication

"Government publication" as used in this chapter, means informational matter which is published as an individual document at Government expense, or as required by law.

1902. Availability of Government publications through Superintendent of Documents; lists of publications not ordered from Government Printing Office

Government publications, except those determined by their issuing components to be required for official use only or for strictly administrative or operational purposes which have no public interest or educational value and publications classified for reasons of national security, shall be made available to depository libraries through the facilities of the Superintendent of Documents for public information. Each component of the Government shall furnish the Superintendent of Documents a list of such publications it issued during the previous month, that were obtained from sources other than the Government Printing Office.

1903. Distribution of publications to depositories; notice to Government components; cost of printing and binding

Upon request of the Superintendent of Documents, components of the Government ordering the printing of publications shall either increase or decrease the number of copies of publications furnished for distribution to designated depository libraries and State libraries so that the number of copies delivered to the Superintendent of Documents is equal to the number of libraries on the list. The number thus delivered may not be restricted by any statutory limitation in force on August 9, 1962. Copies of publications furnished the Superintendent of Documents for distribution to designated depository libraries shall include—

the journal of the Senate and House of Representatives;

all publications, not confidential in character, printed upon the requisition of a congressional committee;

Senate and House public bills and resolutions; and

reports on private bills, concurrent or simple resolutions;

but not so-called cooperative publications which must necessarily be sold in order to be self-sustaining.

The Superintendent of Documents shall currently inform the components of the Government ordering printing of publications as to the number of copies of their publications required for distribution to depository libraries. The cost of printing and binding those publications distributed to depository libraries obtained elsewhere than from the Government Printing Office, shall be borne by components of the Government responsible for their issuance; those requisitioned from the Government Printing Office shall be charged to appropriations provided the Superintendent of Documents for that purpose.

1904. Classified list of Government publications for selection by depositories

The Superintendent of Documents shall currently issue a classified list of Government publications in suitable form, containing annotations of contents and listed by item identification numbers to facilitate the selection of only those publications needed by depository libraries. The selected publications shall be distributed to depository libraries in accordance with regulations of the Superintendent of Documents, as long as they fulfill the conditions provided by law.

1905. Distribution to depositories; designation of additional libraries; justification; authorization for certain designations

The Government publications selected from lists prepared by the

Superintendent of Documents, and when requested from him, shall be distributed to depository libraries specifically designated by law and to libraries designated by Senators, Representatives, and the Resident Commissioner from Puerto Rico, by the Commissioner of the District of Columbia, and by the Governors of Guam, American Samoa, and the Virgin Islands, respectively. Additional libraries within areas served by Representatives or the Resident Commissioner from Puerto Rico may be designated by them to receive Government publications to the extent that the total number of libraries designated by them does not exceed two within each area. Not more than two additional libraries within a State may be designated by each Senator from the State. Before an additional library within a State, congressional district or the Commonwealth of Puerto Rico is designated as a depository for Government publications, the head of that library shall furnish his Senator, Representative, or the Resident Commissioner from Puerto Rico, as the case may be, with justification of the necessity for the additional designation. The justification, which shall also include a certification as to the need for the additional depository library designation, shall be signed by the head of every existing depository library within the congressional district or the Commonwealth of Puerto Rico or by the head of the library authority of the State or the Commonwealth of Puerto Rico, within which the additional depository library is to be located. The justification for additional depository library designations shall be transmitted to the Superintendent of Documents by the Senator, Representative, or the Resident Commissioner from Puerto Rico, as the case may be. The Commissioner of the District of Columbia may designate two depository libraries in the District of Columbia, the Governor of Guam and the Governor of American Samoa may each designate one depository library in Guam and American Samoa, respectively, and the Governor of the Virgin Islands may designate one depository library on the island of Saint Thomas and one on the island of Saint Croix.

1906. Land-grant colleges constituted depositories
Land-grant colleges are constituted depositories to receive Government publications subject to the depository laws.

1907. Libraries of executive departments, service academies, and independent agencies constituted depositories; certifications of need; disposal of unwanted publications
The libraries of the executive departments, of the United States Military Academy, of the United States Naval Academy, of the United

States Air Force Academy, of the United States Coast Guard Academy, and of the United States Merchant Marine Academy are designated depositories of Government publications. A depository library within each independent agency may be designated upon certification of need by the head of the independent agency to the Superintendent of Documents. Additional depository libraries within executive departments and independent agencies may be designated to receive Government publications to the extent that the number so designated does not exceed the number of major bureaus or divisions of the departments and independent agencies. These designations may be made only after certification by the head of each executive department or independent agency to the Superintendent of Documents as to the justifiable need for additional depository libraries. Depository libraries within executive departments and independent agencies may dispose of unwanted Government publications after first offering them to the Library of Congress and the Archivist of the United States.

1908. American Antiquarian Society to receive certain publications

One copy of the public journals of the Senate and of the House of Representatives, and of the documents published under the orders of the Senate and House of Representatives, respectively, shall be transmitted to the Executive of the Commonwealth of Massachusetts for the use and benefit of the American Antiquarian Society of the Commonwealth.

1909. Requirements of depository libraries; reports on conditions; investigations; termination; replacement

Only a library able to provide custody and service for depository materials and located in an area where it can best serve the public need, and within an area not already adequately served by existing depository libraries may be designated by Senators, Representatives, the Resident Commissioner from Puerto Rico, the Commissioner of the District of Columbia, or the Governors of Guam, American Samoa, or the Virgin Islands as a depository of Government publications. The designated depository libraries shall report to the Superintendent of Documents at least every two years concerning their condition.

The Superintendent of Documents shall make firsthand investigation of conditions for which need is indicated and include the results of investigations in his annual report. When he ascertains that the number of books in a depository library is below ten thousand, other than Government publications, or it has ceased to be maintained so as to be accessible to the public, or that the Government publications which have been furnished the library have not been properly maintained, he shall delete the library from the list of depository libraries if the library fails to correct the unsatisfactory conditions within six months. The Representative or the Resident Commissioner from Puerto Rico in whose area the library is located or the Senator who made the designation, or a successor of the Senator, and, in the case of a library in the District of Columbia, the Commissioner of the District of Columbia, and, in the case of a library in Guam, American Samoa, or the Virgin Islands, the Governor, shall be notified and shall then be authorized to designate another library within the area served by him, which shall meet the conditions herein required, but which may not be in excess of the number of depository libraries authorized by law within the State, district, territory, or the Commonwealth of Puerto Rico, as the case may be.

1910. Designations of replacement depositories; limitations on numbers; conditions

The designation of a library to replace a depository library, other than a depository library specifically designated by law, may be made only within the limitations on total numbers specified by section 1905 of this title, and only when the library to be replaced ceases to exist, or when the library voluntarily relinquishes its depository status, or when the Superintendent of Documents determines that it no longer fulfills the conditions provided by law for depository libraries.

1911. Free use of Government publications in depositories; disposal of unwanted publications

Depository libraries shall make Government publications available for the free use of the general public, and may dispose of them after retention for five years under section 1912 of this title, if the depository library is served by a regional depository library. Depository libraries not served by a regional depository library, or that are regional depository libraries themselves, shall retain Government publications permanently in either printed form or in microfacsimile form, except superseded publications or those issued later in bound form which may be discarded as authorized by the Superintendent of Documents.

1912. Regional depositories; designation; functions; disposal of publications

Not more than two depository libraries in each State and the Commonwealth of Puerto Rico may be designated as regional depositories, and shall receive from the Superintendent of Documents copies of all new and revised Government publications authorized for distribution to depository libraries. Designation of regional depository libraries may be made by a Senator or the Resident Commissioner from Puerto Rico within the areas served by them, after approval by the head of the library authority of the State or the Commonwealth of Puerto Rico, as the case may be, who shall first ascertain from the head of the library to be so designated that the library will, in addition to fulfilling the requirements for depository libraries, retain at least one copy of all Government publications either in printed or microfacsimile form (except those authorized to be discarded by the Superintendent of Documents); and within the region served will provide interlibrary loan, reference service, and assistance for depository libraries in the disposal of unwanted Government publications. The agreement to function as a regional depository library shall be transmitted to the Superintendent of Documents by the Senator of the Resident Commissioner from Puerto Rico when the designation is made.

The libraries designated as regional depositories may permit depository libraries, within the areas served by them, to dispose of Government publications which they have retained for five years after first offering them to other depository libraries within their area, then to other libraries.

1913. Appropriations for supplying depository libraries; restriction

Appropriations available for the Office of Superintendent of Documents may not be used to supply depository libraries documents, books, or other printed matter not requested by them, and their requests shall be subject to approval by the Superintendent of Documents.

1914. Implementation of depository library program by Public Printer

The Public Printer, with the approval of the Joint Committee on Printing, as provided by section 103 of this title, may use any measures he considers necessary for the economical and practical implementation of this chapter.

1. Excerpted from *Government Depository Libraries, present laws governing designated depository libraries, Revised Apr. 1971.* 1971. (Joint Committee print, 92nd Congress, 1st session).

2. Excerpted from *Government Depository Libraries, present laws governing designated depository libraries, Revised Apr. 1971.* 1971. (Joint Committee print, 92nd Congress, 1st session).

Appendix VI

List of Depository Libraries as of September 1, 1971

Geographical Location[1]

Alabama

Alexander City	Alexander City State Junior College, Thomas D. Russell Library (1967).
Auburn	Auburn University, Ralph Brown Draughon Library (1907).
Birmingham	Birmingham Public Library (1895).
	Birmingham-Southern College, M. Paul Phillips Library (1932).
	Jefferson State Junior College, James B. Allen Library (1970).
	Samford University, Harwell G. Davis Library (1884).
Enterprise	Enterprise State Junior College Library (1967).
Florence	Florence State University, Comer Library (1932).
Gadsden	Gadsden Public Library (1963).
Huntsville	University of Alabama, Huntsville, Campus Library (1964).
Jacksonville	Jacksonville State University, Romana Wood Library (1929).

Maxwell A.F. Base	Air University Library (1963).
Mobile	Mobile Public Library (1963).
	Spring Hill College, Thomas Byrne Memorial Library (1937).
	University of South Alabama Library (1968).
Montgomery	Alabama State Department of Archives and History Library (1884).
	Alabama Supreme Court Library (1884).
	Auburn University at Montgomery Library (1971).
Normal	Alabama Agricultural and Mechanical College, Drake Memorial Library (1963).
St. Bernard	St. Bernard College Library (1962).
Troy	Troy State University, Lurleen B. Wallace Educational Resources Center (1963).
Tuskegee Institute	Tuskegee Institute, Hollis Burke Grissell Library (1907).
University	University of Alabama Law Library (1967).
	University of Alabama Library (1860). REGIONAL

Alaska

Anchorage	Anchorage Community College Library (1961).
	Anchorage Methodist University Library (1963).
College	University of Alaska Library (1922).
Juneau	Alaska State Library (1964).
Ketchikan	Ketchikan Community College Library (1970).

Arizona

Flagstaff	Northern Arizona University Library (1937).
Phoenix	Department of Library and Archives (unknown) REGIONAL
	Phoenix Public Library (1917)
Prescott	Prescott College Library (1968)
Tempe	Arizona State University, Matthews Library (1944).
Thatcher	Eastern Arizona College Library (1963).
Tucson	Tucson Public Library (1970).
	University of Arizona Library (1907). REGIONAL
Yuma	Yuma City-County Library (1963).

Arkansas

Arkadelphia	Ouachita Baptist University, Riley Library (1963).
Batesville	Arkansas College Library (1963).
Clarksville	College of the Ozarks Library (1925).
College Heights	Arkansas Agricultural and Mechanical College Library (1956).
Conway	Hendrix College, O.C. Bailey Library (1903).
Fayetteville	University of Arkansas Library (1907).
Little Rock	Arkansas Supreme Court Library (1962).
	Little Rock Public Library (1953).
Magnolia	Southern State College, J.M. Peace Library (1956).
Russellville	Arkansas Polytechnic College, Tomlinson Library (1925).
Searcy	Harding College, Beaumont Memorial Library (1963).
State College	Arkansas State University, Dean B. Ellis Library (1913).
Walnut Ridge	Southern Baptist College, Felix Goodson Library (1967).

California

Anaheim	Anaheim Public Library (1963).
Arcata	Humboldt State College Library (1963).
Bakersfield	Kern County Library (1943).
Berkeley	University of California, General Library (1907).
	University of California, Law Library, Earl Warren Legal Center (1963).
Chico	Chico State College Library (1962).
Claremont	Pomona College Documents Collection, Honnold Library (1913).
Culver City	Culver City Library (1966).
Davis	University of California Library (1953).
Downey	Downey City Library (1963).
Fresno	Fresno County Free Library (1920).
	Fresno State College Library (1962).
Fullerton	California State College at Fullerton Library (1963).
Garden Grove	Adult Reference Center Library (1963).
Gardena	Gardena Public Library (1966).
Hayward	California State College at Hayward Library (1963).

Huntington Park	Huntington Park Library, San Antonio Region (1970).
Inglewood	Inglewood Public Library (1963).
Irvine	University of California at Irvine Library (1963).
La Jolla	University of California, San Diego, University Library (1963).
Lakewood	Angelo Iacoboni Public Library (1970).
Lancaster	Lancaster Regional Library (1967).
Long Beach	California State College at Long Beach Library (1962).
	Long Beach Public Library (1933).
Los Angeles	California State College at Los Angeles, John F. Kennedy Memorial Library (1956).
	Los Angeles County Law Library (1963).
	Los Angeles Public Library (1891).
	Loyola University of Los Angeles Library (1933).
	Occidental College, Mary Norton Clapp Library (1941).
	Pepperdine College Library (1963).
	University of California at Los Angeles Library (1932).
	University of California, School of Law Library (1958).
	University of Southern California Library (1933).
Marysville	Yuba College Library (1963).
Menlo Park	Department of the Interior, Geological Survey Library (1962).
Montebello	Montebello Library (1966).
Monterey	Naval Postgraduate School Library (1963).
Monterey Park	Bruggemeyer Memorial Library (1964).
Newhall	Newhall Library of Los Angeles County Public Library System (1967).
Northridge	San Fernando Valley State College Library (1958).
Oakland	Mills College Library (1966).
	Oakland Public Library (1923).
Pasadena	California Institute of Technology, Millikan Memorial Library (1933).
	Pasadena Public Library (1963).
Pleasant Hill	Contra Costa County Library (1964).
Redding	Shasta County Library (1956).
Redlands	University of Redlands Library (1933).
Redwood City	Redwood City Public Library (1966).

Reseda	West Valley Regional Branch Library (1966).
Richmond	Richmond Public Library (1943).
Riverside	Riverside Public Library (1947).
	University of California at Riverside Library (1963).
Sacramento	California State Library (1895). REGIONAL
	Sacramento City Library (1880).
	Sacramento County Law Library (1963).
	Sacramento State College Library (1963).
San Bernardino	San Bernardino County Free Library (1964).
San Diego	San Diego County Library (1966).
	San Diego Public Library (1895).
	San Diego State College Library (1962).
	University of San Diego Law Library (1967).
San Francisco	Mechanics' Institute Library (1889).
	San Francisco Public Library (1889).
	San Francisco State College, Social Science and Business Library (1955).
	University of San Francisco, Richard A. Gleeson Library (1963).
San Jose	San Jose State College Library (1962).
San Leandro	San Leandro Community Library Center (1961).
San Luis Obispo	California State Polytechnic College Library (1969).
Santa Ana	Santa Ana Public Library (1959).
Santa Barbara	University of California at Santa Barbara Library (1960).
Santa Clara	University of Santa Clara, Orradre Library (1963).
Santa Cruz	University of California at Santa Cruz Library (1963).
Santa Rosa	Santa Rosa-Sonoma County Public Library (1896).
Stanford	Stanford University Libraries (1895).
Stockton	Public Library of Stockton and San Joaquin County (1884).
Thousand Oaks	California Lutheran College Library (1964).
Torrance	Torrance Public Library (1969).
Turlock	Stanislaus State College Library (1964).
Van Nuys	Los Angeles Valley College Library (1970).
Visalia	Tulare County Free Library (1967).
Walnut	Mount San Antonio College Library (1966).
West Covina	West Covina Library (1966).
Whittier	Whittier College, Wardman Library (1963).

Canal Zone
Balboa Heights   Canal Zone Library-Museum (1963).

Colorado
Alamosa   Adams State College Library (1963).
Boulder   University of Colorado Libraries (1879). RE-
                     GIONAL
Colorado Springs Colorado College, Charles Leaming Tutt Library
                     (1880).
Denver   Colorado State Library (unknown).
                  Denver Public Library (1884). REGIONAL
                  Department of Interior, Bureau of Reclamation
                     Library (1962).
                  Regis College, Dayton Memorial Library (1915).
                  University of Denver, Mary Reed Library (1909).
Fort Collins   Colorado State University Library (1907).
Golden   Colorado School of Mines, Arthur Lakes Library
                     (1939).
                  Jefferson County Public Library, Bonfils-Stanton
                     Regional Library (1968).
Greeley   University of Northern Colorado Library (1966).
Gunnison   Western State College, Leslie J. Savage Library
                     (1932).
La Junta   Otero Junior College, Wheeler Library (1963).
Pueblo   Pueblo Regional Library (1893).
                  Southern Colorado State College Library (1965).
U.S. Air Force   Academy Library (1956).
   Academy

Connecticut
Bridgeport   Bridgeport Public Library (1884).
Danbury   Western Connecticut State College, Ruth A. Haas
                     Library (1967).
Enfield   Enfield Public Library (1967).
Hartford   Connecticut State Library (unknown). REGIONAL
                  Hartford Public Library (1945).
                  Trinity College Library (1895).
Middletown   Wesleyan University, Olin Library (1906).
Mystic   Marine Historical Association, Inc., Mystic Sea-
                     port Library (1964).
New Haven   Southern Connecticut State College Library (1968).
                  Yale University Library (1859).

New London	Connecticut College Library (1926).
	U.S. Coast Guard Academy Library (1939).
Pomfret	Pomfret School Library (1968).
Storrs	University of Connecticut, Wilbur Cross Library (1907).
Waterbury	Silas Bronson Library (1869).

Delaware

Dover	Delaware State College, William C. Jason Library (1962).
	State Law Library in Kent County (unknown).
Georgetown	Delaware Technical and Community College, Southern Branch Library (1968).
Newark	University of Delaware, Morris Library (1907).
Wilmington	Wilmington Institute Free Library (1861).

District of Columbia

Washington	Civil Service Commission Library (1963).
	Department of Commerce Library (1955).
	Department of Health, Education, and Welfare Library (1954).
	Department of Housing and Urban Development Library (1969).
	Department of the Interior Central Library (1895).
	Department of the Interior, Geological Survey Library (1962).
	Department of Justice Main Library (1895).
	Department of State Library (1895).
	Department of State, Office of Legal Advisor, Law Library (1966).
	Department of Transportation, National Highway Safety Bureau Library (1968).
	District of Columbia Public Library (1943).
	Federal Bureau of Investigation Academy Library (1970).
	Federal City College Library (1970).
	Georgetown University Library (1969).
	Indian Claims Commission Library (1968).
	National Agricultural Library (1895).
	National War College Library (1895).

Navy Department Library (1895).

Navy Department, Office of Judge Advocate General Library (1963).

Office of Management and Budget Library (1965).

Office of the Adjutant General, Department of Army Library (1969).

Post Office Department Library (1895).

Treasury Department Library (1895).

Veterans Administration, Medical and General Reference Library (1967).

Florida

Boca Raton	Florida Atlantic University Library (1963).
Coral Gables	University of Miami Library (1939).
Daytona Beach	Volusia County Public Libraries (1963).
De Land	Stetson University, duPont-Ball Library (1887).
Fort Lauderdale	Fort Lauderdale Public Library (1967).
	Nova University Library (1967).
Gainesville	University of Florida Libraries (1907). REGIONAL
Jacksonville	Haydon Burns Library (1914).
	Jacksonville University, Swisher Library (1962).
Lakeland	Lakeland Public Library (1928).
Leesburg	Lake-Sumter Community College Library (1963).
Melbourne	Florida Institute of Technology Library (1963).
Miami	Florida International University Library (1970).
	Miami-Dade Junior College, North Campus Library (1967).
	Miami Public Library (1952).
Opa Locka	Biscayne College Library (1966).
Orlando	Florida Technological University Library (1966).
Palatka	St. Johns River Junior College Library (1963).
Pensacola	University of West Florida, John C. Pace Library (1966).
St. Petersburg	St. Petersburg Public Library (1965).
Sarasota	Sarasota Public Library (1970).
Tallahassee	Florida Agricultural and Mechanical University, Coleman Memorial Library (1936).
	Florida State Library (1929).
	Florida State University, R.M. Strozier Library (1941).

Tampa	Tampa Public Library (1965).	85
	University of South Florida Library (1962).	APPENDIX VI
	University of Tampa Library (1953).	
Winter Park	Rollins College, Mills Memorial Library (1909).	

Georgia

Albany	Albany Public Library (1964).
Americus	Georgia Southwestern College, Wade Lott Memorial Library (1966).
Athens	University of Georgia Libraries (1907).
Atlanta	Atlanta Public Library (1880).
	Atlanta University, Trevor Arnett Library (1962).
	Emory University, Robert W. Woodruff Library (1928).
	Emory University, School of Law Library (1968).
	Georgia Institute of Technology, Price Gilbert Memorial Library (1963).
	Georgia State Library (unknown).
	Georgia State University Library (1970).
Augusta	Augusta College Library (1962).
Brunswick	Brunswick Public Library (1965).
Carrollton	West Georgia College, Sanford Library (1962).
Dahlonega	North Georgia College Library (1939).
Gainesville	Chestatee Regional Library (1968).
Macon	Mercer University Library (1964).
Marietta	Kennesaw Junior College Library (1968).
Milledgeville	Georgia College at Milledgeville, Ina Dillard Russell Library (1950).
Mount Berry	Berry College, Memorial Library (1970).
Savannah	Savannah Public and Chatham-Effingham Liberty Regional Library (1857).
Statesboro	Georgia Southern College, Rosenwald Library (1939).
Valdosta	Valdosta State College, Richard Holmes Powell Library (1956).

Guam

Agana	Nieves M. Flores Memorial Library (1962).

Hawaii

Hilo	University of Hawaii, Hilo Campus Library (1962).
Honolulu	Chaminade College of Honolulu Library (1965).

Hawaii Medical Library, Inc. (1968).
Hawaii State Library (1929).
Municipal Reference Library of the City and County of Honolulu (1965).
University of Hawaii Library (1907).

Laie	Church College of Hawaii Library (1964).
Lihue	Kauai Public Library (1967).
Pearl City	Leeward Community College Library (1967).
Wailuku	Maui Public Library (1962).

Idaho

Boise	Boise State College Library (1966).
	Boise Public Library (1929).
	Idaho State Law Library (unknown).
	Idaho State Library (1971).
Burley	Burley Public Library (1970)
Caldwell	College of Idaho, Terteling Library (1930).
Moscow	University of Idaho Library (1907). REGIONAL
Pocatello	Idaho State University Library (1908).
Rexburg	Ricks College, David O. McKay Library (1946).
Twin Falls	College of Southern Idaho Library (1970).

Illinois

Bloomington	Illinois Wesleyan University Libraries (1964).
Carbondale	Southern Illinois University Library (1932).
Carlinville	Blackburn College Library (1954).
Carterville	Shawnee Library System (1971).
Champaign	University of Illinois Law Library, College of Law (1965).
Charleston	Eastern Illinois University, Booth Library (1962).
Chicago	Field Museum of Natural History Library (1963).
	Chicago Public Library (1876).
	Chicago State College Library (1954).
	John Crerar Library (1909).
	Loyola University, E.M. Cudahy Memorial Library (1966).
	Newberry Library (1890).
	Northeastern Illinois University Library (1961).
	University of Chicago Law Library (1964).
	University of Chicago Library (1897).
	University of Illinois, Chicago Circle Campus Library (1957).

Decatur	Decatur Public Library (1954).
De Kalb	Northern Illinois University, Swen Franklin Parson Library (1960).
Edwardsville	Southern Illinois University, Lovejoy Memorial Library (1959).
Elsah	Principia College, Marshall Brooks Library (1957).
Evanston	Northwestern University Library (1905).
Freeport	Freeport Public Library (1905).
Galesburg	Galesburg Public Library (1896).
Jacksonville	MacMurry College, Henry Pfeiffer Library (1929).
Kankakee	Olivet Nazarene College, Memorial Library (1946).
Lake Forest	Lake Forest College, Donnelley Library (1962).
Lebanon	McKendree College, Holman Library (1968).
Lisle	St. Procopius College, Theodore F. Lownik Library (1911).
Lockport	Lewis College of Science and Technology Library (1952).
Macomb	Western Illinois University Memorial Library (1962).
Moline	Black Hawk College, Learning Resources Center (1970).
Monmouth	Monmouth College Library (1860).
Normal	Illinois State University, Milner Library (1877).
Oak Park	Oak Park Public Library (1963).
Peoria	Bradley University, Cullom Davis Library (1963). Peoria Public Library (1883).
River Forest	Rosary College Library (1966).
Rockford	Rockford Public Library (unknown).
Springfield	Illinois State Library (unknown). REGIONAL
Urbana	University of Illinois Library (1907).
Wheaton	Wheaton College Library (1964).
Woodstock	Woodstock Public Library (1963).

Indiana

Anderson	Anderson College, Charles E. Wilson Library (1959).
Bloomington	Indiana University Library (1881).
Crawfordsville	Wabash College, Lilly Library (1906).
Evansville	Evansville and Vanderburgh County Public Library (1928).

	Indiana State University, Evansville Campus Library (1969).
Fort Wayne	Indiana-Purdue Universities, Regional Campus Library (1965).
	Public Library of Fort Wayne and Allen County (unknown).
Gary	Gary Public Library (1943).
	Indiana University, Northwest Campus Library (1966).
Greencastle	De Pauw University, Roy O. West Library (1879).
Hammond	Hammond Public Library (1964).
Hanover	Hanover College Library (1892).
Huntington	Huntington College Library (1964).
Indianapolis	Butler University, Irwin Library (1965).
	Indiana State Library (unknown). REGIONAL
	Indiana University, Law Library (1967).
	Indianapolis Public Library (1906).
Jeffersonville	Indiana University, Southeastern Campus Library (1965).
Kokomo	Indiana University, Kokomo Regional Campus Library (1969).
Lafayette	Purdue University Library (1907).
Muncie	Ball State University Library (1959).
	Muncie Public Library (1906).
Notre Dame	University of Notre Dame, Memorial Library (1883).
Rensselaer	St. Joseph's College Library (1964).
Richmond	Earlham College, Lilly Library (1964).
	Morrison-Reeves Library (1906).
South Bend	Indiana University, South Bend-Mishawaka Campus Library (1965).
Terre Haute	Indiana State University, Cunningham Memorial Library (1906).
Valparaiso	Valparaiso University, Moellering Memorial Library (1930).

Iowa

Ames	Iowa State University of Science and Technology Library (1907).
Cedar Falls	University of Northern Iowa Library (1946).
Council Bluffs	Free Public Library (1885).

Loyola University Library (1942).

New Orleans Public Library (1883).

Southern University in New Orleans Library (1962).

Tulane University, Howard-Tilton Memorial Library (1942).

Pineville   Louisiana College, Richard W. Norton Memorial Library (1969).

Ruston   Louisiana Polytechnic Institute Library (1896). REGIONAL

Shreveport   Louisiana State University at Shreveport Library (1967).

Shreve Memorial Library (1923).

Thibodaux   Francis T. Nicholls State College, Leonidas Polk Library (1962).

Maine

Augusta   Maine State Library (unknown).

Bangor   Bangor Public Library (1884).

Brunswick   Bowdoin College, Hawthorne-Longfellow Library (1884).

Castine   Maine Maritime Academy, Nutting Memorial Library (1969).

Lewiston   Bates College Library (1883).

Orono   University of Maine, Raymond H. Fogler Library (1907). REGIONAL

Portland   Portland Public Library (1884).

University of Maine Law Library (1964).

Springvale   Nasson College Library (1961).

Waterville   Colby College Library (1884).

Maryland

Annapolis   Maryland State Library (unknown).

U.S. Naval Academy Library (1895).

Baltimore   Enoch Pratt Free Library (1887).

Johns Hopkins University, Milton S. Eisenhower Library (1882).

Morgan State College, Soper Library (1940).

University of Maryland, School of Law Library (1969).

Bel Air   Harford Junior College Library (1967).

Bethseda	Montgomery County Department of Public Libraries (1951).
Chestertown	Washington College, Chester M. Miller Library (1891).
College Park	University of Maryland, McKeldin Library (1925). REGIONAL
Frostburg	Frostburg State College, Jerome Framptom Library (1967).
Germantown	Atomic Energy Commission Library (1963).
Patuxent River	Naval Air Station Library (1968).
Salisbury	Salisbury State College, Blackwell Library (1965).
Towson	Goucher College, Julia Rogers Library (1966).
Westminster	Western Maryland College Library (1896).

Massachusetts

Amherst	Amherst College Library (1884).
	University of Massachusetts, Goodell Library (1907).
Belmont	Belmont Memorial Library (1968).
Boston	Boston Athenaeum Library (unknown).
	Boston College, Bapst Library (1963).
	Boston Public Library (1859). REGIONAL
	Northeastern University, Dodge Library (1962).
	State Library of Massachusetts (unknown).
Brookline	Public Library of Brookline (1925).
Cambridge	Harvard College Library (1860).
	Massachusetts Institute of Technology Libraries (1946).
Chicopee	Our Lady of the Elms College Library (1969).
Lowell	Lowell Technological Institute Library (1952).
Lynn	Lynn Public Library (1953).
Marlborough	Marlborough Public Library (1971).
Medford	Tufts University Library (1899).
New Bedford	New Bedford Free Public Library (1858).
North Dartmouth	Southeastern Massachusetts University Library (1965).
North Easton	Stonehill College, Cushing-Martin Library (1962).
Springfield	Springfield City Library (1966).
Waltham	Brandeis University, Goldfarb Library (1965).
Wellesley	Wellesley College Library (1943).
Wenham	Gordon College, Winn Library (1963).
Williamstown	Williams College Library (unknown).

Wilmington	Wilmington Memorial Library (1971).
Worcester	American Antiquarian Society Library (1814).
	Worcester Public Library (1859).

Michigan

Albion	Albion College, Stockwell Memorial Library (1966).
Allendale	Grand Valley State College Library (1963).
Alma	Alma College, Monteith Library (1963).
Ann Arbor	Great Lakes Basin Library (1971).
	University of Michigan, General Library (1884).
Battle Creek	Willard Library (1876).
Benton Harbor	Benton Harbor Public Library (1907).
Bloomfield Hills	Cranbrook Institute of Science Library (1940).
Dearborn	Henry Ford Centennial Library (1969).
	Henry Ford Community College Library (1957).
Detroit	Detroit Public Library (1868). REGIONAL
	Marygrove College Library (1965).
	Mercy College of Detroit Library (1965).
	University of Detroit Library (1884).
	Wayne County Public Library (1957).
	Wayne State University Library (1937).
East Lansing	Michigan State University, Law Library (1971).
	Michigan State University Library (1907).
Escanaba	Michigan State Library, Upper Peninsula Branch (1964).
Farmington	Martin Luther King Learning Resources Center, Oakland Community College (1968).
Flint	Charles Stewart Mott Library (1959).
	Flint Public Library (1967).
Grand Rapids	Grand Rapids Public Library (1876).
	Knollcrest Calvin Library (1967).
Houghton	Michigan Technological University Library (1876).
Jackson	Jackson Public Library (1965).
Kalamazoo	Kalamazoo Library System (1907).
	Western Michigan University, Dwight B. Waldo Library (1963).
Lansing	Michigan State Library (unknown). REGIONAL
Livonia	Schoolcraft College Library (1962).
Marquette	Northern Michigan University, Olsen Library (1963).
Mt. Clemens	Macomb County Library (1968).

Mt. Pleasant	Central Michigan University Library (1958).
Muskegon	Hackley Public Library (1894).
Petoskey	North Central Michigan College Library (1962).
Port Huron	Saint Clair County Library System (1876).
Rochester	Oakland University, Kresge Library (1964).
Saginaw	Hoyt Public Library (1890).
Traverse City	Northwestern Michigan College, Mark Osterlin Library (1964).
University Center	Delta College Library (1963).
Ypsilanti	Eastern Michigan University Library (1965).

Minnesota

Bemidji	Bemidji State College, A.C. Clark Library (1963).
Collegeville	St. John's University, Alcuin Library (1954).
Duluth	Duluth Public Library (1909).
Mankato	Mankato State College Memorial Library (1962).
Minneapolis	Anoka County Library (1971).
	Hennepin County Public Library (1971).
	Minneapolis Public Library (1893).
	University of Minnesota, Wilson Library (1907). REGIONAL
Moorhead	Moorhead State College Library (1956).
Morris	University of Minnesota at Morris Library (1963).
Northfield	Carleton College Library (1930).
	St. Olaf College, Rolvaag Memorial Library (1930).
St. Cloud	St. Cloud State College Library (1962).
St. Paul	Minnesota Historical Society Library (1867).
	Minnesota State Law Library (unknown).
	St. Paul Public Library (1914).
Saint Peter	Gustavus Adolphus College Library (1941).
Stillwater	Stillwater Public Library (1893).
Willmar	Kandiyohi County-Willmar Library (1958).
Winona	Winona State College, Maxwell Library (1969).

Mississippi

Columbus	Mississippi State College for Women, J.C. Fant Memorial Library (1929).
Hattiesburg	University of Southern Mississippi Library (1935).
Jackson	Jackson State College Library (1968).

	Millsaps College, Millsaps-Wilson Library (1963).
	Mississippi Library Commission (1947).
	Mississippi State Law Library (unknown).
Lorman	Alcorn Agricultural and Mechanical College Library (1970).
State College	Mississippi State University, Mitchell Memorial Library (1907).
University	University of Mississippi Library (1883).
	University of Mississippi, School of Law Library (1967).

Missouri

Cape Girardeau	Southeast Missouri State College, Kent Library (1916).
Columbia	University of Missouri Library (1862).
Fayette	Central Methodist College Library (1962).
Fulton	Westminster College, Reeves Library (1875).
Jefferson City	Lincoln University, Inman E. Page Library (1944).
	Missouri State Library (1963).
	Missouri Supreme Court Library (unknown).
Joplin	Missouri Southern State College Library (1966).
Kansas City	Kansas City Public Library (1881).
	Rockhurst College Library (1917).
	University of Missouri at Kansas City, General Library (1938).
Kirksville	Northeast Missouri State Teachers College, Pickler Memorial Library (1966).
Liberty	William Jewell College Library (1900).
Rolla	University of Missouri at Rolla Library (1907).
St. Joseph	St. Joseph Public Library (1891).
St. Louis	St. Louis County Library (1970).
	St. Louis Public Library (1866).
	St. Louis University, Law Library (1967).
	St. Louis University, Pius XII Memorial Library (1866).
	University of Missouri at St. Louis Library (1966).
	Washington University, John M. Olin Library (1906).
Springfield	Drury College Library (1874).
	Southwest Missouri State College Library (1963).
Warrensburg	Central Missouri State College, Ward Edwards Library (1914).

Montana

Billings	Eastern Montana College Library (1924).
Bozeman	Montana State University Library (1907).
Butte	Montana College of Mineral Science and Technology Library (1901).
Helena	Montana Historical Society Library (unknown).
	Montana State Library (1966).
Missoula	University of Montana Library (1909). REGIONAL

Nebraska

Blair	Dana College Library (1924).
Crete	Doane College, Whitin Library (1944).
Fremont	Midland Lutheran College Library (1924).
Kearney	Kearney State College, Calvin T. Ryan Library (1962).
Lincoln	Nebraska State Library (unknown).
	University of Nebraska, Don L. Love Memorial Library (1907).
Omaha	Creighton University, Alumni Library (1964).
	Omaha Public Library (1880).
	University of Omaha, Gene Eppley Library (1939).
Scottsbluff	Scottsbluff Public Library (1925).
Wayne	Wayne State College, U.S. Conn Library (1970).

Nevada

Carson City	Nevada State Library (unknown).
Las Vegas	University of Nevada at Las Vegas, James R. Dickinson Library (1959).
Reno	University of Nevada Library (1907). REGIONAL

New Hampshire

Concord	New Hampshire State Library (unknown).
Durham	University of New Hampshire Library (1907).
Hanover	Dartmouth College, Baker Library (1884).
Henniker	New England College Library (1966).
Manchester	Manchester City Library (1884).
	St. Anselm's College, Geisel Library (1693).

New Jersey

Atlantic City	Atlantic City Free Public Library (1908).
Bayonne	Bayonne Free Public Library (1909).

Bloomfield	Free Public Library of Bloomfield (1965).
Bridgeton	Cumberland County Library (1966).
Camden	Rutgers University-Camden Library (1966).
Convent Station	College of St. Elizabeth, Mahoney Library (1938).
East Orange	East Orange Public Library (1966).
Elizabeth	Free Public Library of Elizabeth (1895).
Glassboro	Glassboro State College, Savitz Library (1963).
Hackensack	Johnson Free Public Library (1966).
Irvington	Free Public Library of Irvington (1966).
Jersey City	Jersey City Public Library (1879).
	Jersey City State College, Forrest A. Irvin Library (1963).
Madison	Drew University, Rose Memorial Library (1939).
Mahwah	Ramapo College Library (1971).
Mount Holly	Burlington County Area Library (1966).
New Brunswick	Free Public Library (1908).
	Rutgers University Library (1907).
Newark	Newark Public Library (1906). REGIONAL
	Rutgers-The State University, John Cotton Dana Library (1966).
Passaic	Passaic Public Library (1964).
Plainfield	Plainfield Public Library (1971).
Princeton	Princeton University Library (1884).
Rutherford	Fairleigh Dickinson University, Messler Library (1953).
Shrewsbury	Monmouth County Library (1968).
South Orange	Seton Hall University Library (1947).
Teaneck	Fairleigh Dickinson University, Teaneck Campus Library (1963).
Toms River	Ocean County College Library (1966).
Trenton	New Jersey State Library, Law and Reference Bureau, Department of Education (unknown).
	Trenton Free Public Library (1902).
Upper Montclair	Montclair State College, Harry A. Sprague Library (1967).
West Long Branch	Monmouth College, Guggenheim Memorial Library (1963).
Woodbridge	Free Public Library of Woodbridge (1965).

New Mexico

Albuquerque	University of New Mexico, Zimmerman Library (1896). REGIONAL

Hobbs	New Mexico Junior College, Pannell Library (1969).
Las Cruces	New Mexico State University Library (1907).
Las Vegas	New Mexico Highlands University, Donnelly Library (1913).
Portales	Eastern New Mexico University Library (1962).
Sante Fe	New Mexico State Library (1960). REGIONAL
	Supreme Court Law Library (unknown).

New York

Albany	New York State Library (unknown). REGIONAL
	State University of New York at Albany Library (1964).
Binghamton	State University of New York at Binghamton Library (1962).
Brockport	State University of New York, Drake Memorial Library (1967).
Bronx	Herbert H. Lehman College Library (1967).
Bronxville	Sarah Lawrence College Library (1969).
Brooklyn	Brooklyn College Library (1936).
	Brooklyn Public Library (1908).
	Polytechnic Institute of Brooklyn, Spicer Library (1963).
	Pratt Institute Library (1891).
	State University of New York, Downstate Medical Center Library (1958).
Buffalo	Buffalo and Erie County Public Library (1895).
	State University of New York at Buffalo, Lockwood Memorial Library (1963).
Canton	St. Lawrence University, Owen D. Young Library (1920).
Corning	Corning Community College, Arthur A. Houghton, Jr. Library (1963).
Cortland	State University of New York, College at Cortland, Memorial Library (1964).
Delhi	State University Agricultural and Technical College Library (1970).
Douglaston	Cathedral College Library (1971).
Elmira	Elmira College, Gannett-Tripp Learning Center (1956).
Farmingdale	State University Agricultural and Technical Institute at Farmingdale Library (1917).

Flushing	Queens College, Paul Klapper Library (1939).
Garden City	Adelphi University, Swirbul Library (1966).
	Nassau Library System (1965).
Geneseo	State University College, Milne Library (1967).
Greenvale	C.W. Post College Library (1964).
Hamilton	Colgate University Library (1902).
Hempstead	Hofstra University Library (1964).
Huntington	Huntington Public Library (1966).
Ithaca	Cornell University Library (1907).
	New York State Colleges of Agriculture and Home Economics, Albert R. Mann Library (1943).
Jamaica	Queens Borough Public Library (1926).
	St. John's University Library (1956).
Kings Point	U.S. Merchant Marine Academy Library (1962).
Mount Vernon	Mount Vernon Public Library (1962).
New Paltz	State University College Library (1965).
New York City	City University of New York, City College Library (1884).
	College of Insurance, Ecker Library (1965).
	Columbia University Libraries (1882).
	Cooper Union Library (1930).
	Fordham University Library (1937).
	New York Law Institute Library (1909).
	New York Public Library (Astor Branch) (1907).
	New York Public Library (Lenox Branch) (1884).
	New York University Libraries (1967).
	New York University, University Heights Gould Memorial Library (1902).
	State University of New York, Maritime College Library (1947).
Newburgh	Newburgh Free Library (1909).
Oakdale	Dowling College Library (1965).
Oneonta	State University College, James M. Milne Library (1966).
Oswego	State University College, Penfield Library (1966).
Plattsburgh	State University College, Benjamin F. Feinberg Library (1967).
Potsdam	Clarkson College of Technology, Harriet Call Burnap Memorial Library (1938).
	State University College, Frederick W. Crumb Memorial Library (1964).
Poughkeepsie	Vassar College Library (1943).

Purchase	State University of New York, College at Purchase Library (1969).
Rochester	Rochester Public Library (1963).
	University of Rochester Library (1880).
St. Bonaventure	St. Bonaventure College, Friedsam Memorial Library (1938).
Saratoga Springs	Skidmore College Library (1964).
Schenectady	Union College, Schaffer Library (1901).
Staten Island (Grymes Hill)	Wagner College, Horrmann Library (1953).
Stony Brook	State University of New York at Stony Brook Library (1963).
Syracuse	Syracuse University Library (1878).
Troy	Troy Public Library (1869).
Utica	Utica Public Library (1885).
West Point	U.S. Military Academy Library (unknown).
Yonkers	Yonkers Public Library (1910).

North Carolina

Asheville	University of North Carolina at Asheville, D. Hiden Ramsey Library (1965).
Boone	Appalachian State University, Dauphin Disco Dougherty Library (1963).
Buies Creek	Campbell College, Carrie Rich Memorial Library (1965).
Chapel Hill	University of North Carolina Library (1884). REGIONAL
Charlotte	Public Library of Charlotte and Mecklenburg County (1964).
	Queens College, Everett Library (1927).
	University of North Carolina at Charlotte, Arkins Library (1964).
Cullowhee	Western Carolina University, Hunter Library (1953).
Davidson	Davidson College, Hugh A. & Jane Grey Memorial Library (1893).
Durham	Duke University Library (1890).
Fayetteville	Fayetteville State University, Chesnutt Library (1971).
Greensboro	North Carolina Agricultural and Technical State University, F.D. Bluford Library (1937).

	University of North Carolina at Greensboro, Walter Clinton Jackson Library (1963).
Greenville	East Carolina University, J.Y. Joyner Library (1951).
Laurinburg	St. Andrews Presbyterian College, Detamble Library (1969).
Lexington	Davidson County Public Library System (1971).
Murfreesboro	Chowan College, Whitaker Library (1963).
Pembroke	Pembroke State University Library (1965).
Raleigh	North Carolina State Library (unknown).
	North Carolina State University, D.H. Hill Library (1923).
	Wake County Public Libraries (1969).
Rocky Mount	North Carolina Wesleyan College Library (1969).
Salisbury	Catawba College Library (1925).
Wilmington	University of North Carolina at Wilmington, William M. Randall Library (1965).
Wilson	Atlantic Christian College, Clarence L. Hardy Library (1930).
Winston-Salem	Forsyth County Public Library System (1954).
	Wake Forest University, Z. Smith Reynolds Library (1902).

North Dakota

Bismark	North Dakota State Historical Society Library (1907).
	North Dakota State Law Library (unknown).
	State Library Commission Library (1971).
	Veterans Memorial Public Library (1967).
Dickinson	Dickinson State College Library (1968).
Fargo	Fargo Public Library (1964).
	North Dakota State University Library (1907). REGIONAL
Grand Forks	University of North Dakota, Chester Fritz Library (1890).
Minot	Minot State College, Memorial Library (1925).
Valley City	State College Library (1913).

Ohio

Ada	Ohio Northern University, J.P. Taggart Law Library (1965).
Akron	Akron Public Library (1952).

	University of Akron Library (1963).
Alliance	Mount Union College Library (1888).
Ashland	Ashland College Library (1938).
Athens	Ohio University Library (1886).
Bluffton	Bluffton College, Musselman Library (1951).
Bowling Green	Bowling Green State University Library (1933).
Canton	Malone College Library (1970).
Chardon	Geauga County Public Library (1971).
Cincinnati	Public Library of Cincinnati and Hamilton County (1884).
	University of Cincinnati Library (1929).
Cleveland	Case Western Reserve University, Freiberger Library (1913).
	Cleveland Heights-University Heights Public Library (1970).
	Cleveland Public Library (1886).
	Cleveland State University Library (1966).
	John Carroll University, Grasselli Library (1963).
	Municipal Reference Library (1970).
Columbus	Capital University Library (1968).
	Columbus Public Library (1885).
	Ohio State Library (unknown). REGIONAL
	Ohio State University Library (1907).
Dayton	Dayton and Montgomery County Public Library (1909).
	University of Dayton, Albert Emanuel Library (1969).
	Wright State University Library (1965).
Delaware	Ohio Wesleyan University, L.A. Beeghly Library (1845).
Elyria	Elyria Public Library (1966).
Findlay	Findlay College, Shafer Library (1969).
Gambier	Kenyon College Library (1873).
Granville	Denison University Library (1884).
Hiram	Hiram College, Teachout-Price Memorial Library (1874).
Kent	Kent State University Library (1962).
Mansfield	Ohio State University, Mansfield Campus Library (1969).
Marietta	Marietta College, Dawes Memorial Library (1884).
Middletown	Miami University at Middletown, Gardner-Harvey Library (1970).

New Concord	Muskingum College Library (1966).
Oberlin	Oberlin College Library (1858).
Oxford	Miami University, Alumni Library (1909).
Portsmouth	Portsmouth Public Library (unknown).
Rio Grande	Rio Grande College, Jeanette Albiez Davis Library (1966).
Springfield	Warder Public Library (1884).
Steubenville	Public Library of Steubenville and Jefferson County (1950).
Tiffin	Heidelberg College, Beeghly Library (1964).
Toledo	Toledo Public Library (1884).
	University of Toledo Library (1963).
Van Wert	Brumback Library of Van Wert County (1900).
Westerville	Otterbein College, Centennial Library (1967).
Wooster	College of Wooster, the Andrews Library (1966).
Youngstown	Public Library of Youngstown and Mahoning County (1923).
	Youngstown State University Library (1971).

Oklahoma

Ada	East Central State College, Linschcid Library (1914).
Alva	Northwestern State College Library (1907).
Bartlesville	Bureau of Mines, Petroleum Research Center Library (1962).
Durant	Southeastern State College Library (1929).
Edmond	Central State University Library (1934).
Enid	Public Library of Enid and Garfield County (1908).
Langston	Langston University, G. Lamar Harrison Library (1941).
Muskogee	Muskogee Public Library (1971).
Norman	University of Oklahoma Libraries (1893).
Oklahoma City	Oklahoma City University Library (1963).
	Oklahoma Department of Libraries (1893). REGIONAL
Shawnee	Oklahoma Baptist University Library (1933).
Stillwater	Oklahoma State University Library (1907).
Tahlequah	Northeastern State College, John Vaughan Library (1923).
Tulsa	Tulsa City-County Library Commission (1963).
	University of Tulsa, McFarlin Library (1929).
Weatherford	Southwestern State College Library (1958).

Oregon

Ashland	Southern Oregon College Library (1953).
Corvallis	Oregon State University Livrary (1907).
Eugene	University of Oregon Library (1883).
Forest Grove	Pacific University Library (1897).
La Grande	Eastern Oregon College, Walter M. Pierce Library (1954).
McMinnville	Linfield College, Northup Library (1965).
Monmouth	Oregon College of Education Library (1967).
Portland	Department of the Interior, Bonneville Power Administration Library (1962).
	Lewis and Clark College, Aubrey R. Watzek Library (1967).
	Library Association of Portland (1884).
	Portland State University Library (1963).
	Reed College Library (1912).
Salem	Oregon State Library (unknown).
	Willamette University Library (1969).

Pennsylvania

Allentown	Muhlenberg College, Haas Library (1939).
Altoona	Altoona Public Library (1969).
Bethlehem	Lehigh University, Linderman Library (1876).
Carlisle	Dickinson College Library (1947).
Cheyney	Cheyney State College, Leslie Pinckney Hill Library (1947).
Collegeville	Ursinus College Library (1963).
Doylestown	Bucks County Free Library, Center County Library (1970).
East Stroudsburg	East Stroudsburg State College, Kemp Library (1966).
Erie	Erie Public Library (1897).
Greenville	Thiel College, Langenheim Memorial Library (1963).
Harrisburg	State Library of Pennsylvania (unknown). REGIONAL
Haverford	Haverford College Library (1897).
Hazleton	Hazleton Area Public Library (1964).
Indiana	Indiana University of Pennsylvania, Rhodes R. Stabley Library (1962).
Johnstown	Cambria Public Library (1965).

Lancaster	Franklin and Marshall College, Fackenthal Library (1895).
Lewisburg	Bucknell University, Ellen Clarke Bertrand Library (1963).
Mansfield	Mansfield State College Library (1968).
Meadville	Allegheny College, Reis Library (1907).
Millersville	Millersville State College, Ganser Library (1966).
Monessen	Monessen Public Library (1969).
New Castle	New Castle Free Public Library (1963).
Newtown	Bucks County Community College Library (1968).
Norristown	Montgomery County-Norristown Public Library (1969).
Philadelphia	Drexel Institute of Technology Library (1963).
	Free Library of Philadelphia (1897).
	Temple University Library, Serials Records Unit (1947).
	University of Pennsylvania Library (1886).
Pittsburgh	Bureau of Mines, Pittsburgh Research Center Library (1962).
	Carnegie Library of Pittsburgh, Allegheny Regional Branch (1924).
	Carnegie Library of Pittsburgh (1895).
	University of Pittsburgh, Hillman Library (1910).
Pottsville	Pottsville Free Public Library (1967).
Reading	Reading Public Library (1901).
Scranton	Scranton Public Library (1895).
Slippery Rock	Slippery Rock State College, Maltby Library (1965).
Swarthmore	Swarthmore College Library (1923).
University Park	Pennsylvania State University Library (1907).
Villanova	Villanova University, School of Law Library (1964).
Warren	Warren Library Association, Warren Public Library (1885).
Washington	Washington and Jefferson College, Memorial Library (1884).
Waynesburg	Waynesburg College Library (1964).
West Chester	West Chester State College, Francis Harvey Green Library (1967).
Wilkes-Barre	King's College Library (1949).
Williamsport	Lycoming College Library (1970).
York	York Junior College Library (1963).

Puerto Rico

Mayaguez	University of Puerto Rico, Mayaguez Campus Library (1928).
Ponce	Catholic University of Puerto Rico Library (1966).
Rio Piedras	University of Puerto Rico General Library (1928).

Rhode Island

Kingston	University of Rhode Island Library (1907).
Newport	Naval War College Library (1963).
Providence	Brown University, John D. Rockefeller, Jr. Library (unknown).
	Providence College Library (1969).
	Providence Public Library (1884).
	Rhode Island College Library (1965).
	Rhode Island State Library (before 1895).
Warwick	Warwick Public Library (1966).
Westerly	Westerly Public Library (1909).

South Carolina

Charleston	Baptist College at Charleston Library (1967).
	College of Charleston Library (1869).
	The Citadel Memorial Library (1962).
Clemson	Clemson University Library (1893).
Columbia	Benedict College, Starks Library (1969).
	Columbia College Library (1966).
	South Carolina State Library (before 1895).
	University of South Carolina, McKissick Memorial Library (1884).
DueWest	Erskine College, McCain Library (1968).
Florence	Florence County Library (1967).
	Francis Marion College Library (1970).
Greenville	Furman University Library (1962).
	Greenville County Library (1966).
Greenwood	Lander College Library (1967).
Orangeburg	South Carolina State College Whittaker Library (1953).
Rock Hill	Winthrop College Library (1896).
Spartanburg	Spartanburg County Public Library (1967).

South Dakota

Aberdeen	Northern State College Library (1963).

Brookings	South Dakota State University, Lincoln Memorial Library (1889).
Rapid City	Rapid City Public Library (1963).
	South Dakota School of Mines and Technology Library (1963).
Sioux Falls	Augustana College, Mikkelsen Library and Learning Resources Center (1969).
	Carnegie Free Public Library (1903).
Spearfish	Black Hills State College Library (1942).
Vermillion	University of South Dakota, I.D. Weeks Library (1889).
Yankton	Yankton College, Corliss Lay Library (1904).

Tennessee

Bristol	King College Library (1970).
Chattanooga	Chattanooga Public Library (1907).
Clarksville	Austin Peay State University Library (1945).
Cookeville	Tennessee Technological University, Jere Whitson Memorial Library (1969).
Jackson	Lambuth College, Luther L. Gobbel Library (1967).
Jefferson City	Carson-Newman College, Maples Library (1964).
Johnson City	East Tennessee State University, Sherrod Library (1942).
Knoxville	University of Tennessee Law Library (1971).
	University of Tennessee Library (1907).
Martin	University of Tennessee at Martin Library (1957).
Memphis	Memphis Public Library and Information Center (1896).
	Memphis State University, John W. Brister Library (1966).
Morristown	Morristown College, Carnegie Library (1970).
Murfreesboro	Middle Tennessee State University, Andrew L. Todd Library (1912).
Nashville	Fisk Uiversity Library (1965).
	Joint University Libraries (1884).
	Public Library of Nashville and Davidson County (1884).
	Tennessee State Library and Archives, State Library Division (unknown).
Sewanee	University of the South, Jesse Ball duPont Library (1873).

Texas

Abilene	Hardin-Simmons University Library (1940).
Arlington	Arlington Public Library (1970).
	University of Texas at Arlington Library (1963).
Austin	Texas State Library (unknown). REGIONAL
	University of Texas Library (1884).
	University of Texas, Lyndon B. Johnson School of Public Affairs Library (1966).
	University of Texas, School of Law Library (1965).
Baytown	Lee College Library (1970).
Beaumont	Lamar State College of Technology Library (1957).
Brownwood	Howard Payne College, Walker Memorial Library (1964).
Canyon	West Texas State University Library (1928).
College Station	Texas Agricultural and Mechanical University Library (1907).
Commerce	East Texas State University Library (1937).
Corsicana	Navarro Junior College Library (1965).
Dallas	Bishop College, Zale Library (1966).
	Dallas Baptist College Library (1967).
	Dallas Public Library (1900).
	Southern Methodist University, Fondren Library (1925).
Denton	North Texas State University Library (1948).
Edinburg	Pan American College Library (1959).
El Paso	El Paso Public Library (1906).
	University of Texas at El Paso Library (1966).
Fort Worth	Fort Worth Public Library (1905).
	Texas Christian University, Mary Couts Burnett Library (1916).
Freeport	Brazosport Junior College Library (1969).
Galveston	Rosenberg Library (1909).
Houston	Houston Public Library (1884).
	Rice University, Fondren Library (1967).
	University of Houston Library (1957).
Huntsville	Sam Houston State University, Estill Library (1949).
Kingsville	Texas Arts and Industries University Library (1944).
Laredo	Laredo Junior College (1970).
Longview	Nicholson Memorial Public Library (1961).

Lubbock	Texas Tech University Library (1935). REGIONAL.
Marshall	Wiley College, Cole Library (1962).
Nacogdoches	Stephen F. Austin State University, Paul L. Boynton Library (1965).
Plainview	Wayland Baptist College, Van Howeling Memorial Library (1963).
San Angelo	Angelo State University Library (1964).
San Antonio	San Antonio Public Library, Business and Science Department (1899).
	St. Mary's University Library (1964).
	Trinity University Library (1964).
San Marcos	Southwest Texas State University Library (1955).
Seguin	Texas Lutheran College, Blumberg Memorial Library (1970).
Sherman	Austin College, Arthur Hopkins Library (1963).
Texarkana	Texarkana College Library (1963).
Waco	Baylor University Library (1905).
Wichita Falls	Midwestern University, Moffett Library (1963).

Utah

Cedar City	Southern Utah State College Library (1964).
Ephraim	Snow College Library (1963).
Logan	Utah State University, Merrill Library (1907). REGIONAL
Ogden	Weber State College Library (1962).
Provo	Brigham Young University Library (1908).
Salt Lake City	University of Utah, Law Library (1966).
	University of Utah, Medical Sciences Library (1970).
	University of Utah Library (1893).
	Utah State Library Commission, Documents Library (unknown).

Vermont

Burlington	University of Vermont, Bailey Library (1907).
Castleton	Castleton State College, Calvin Coolidge Library (1969).
Johnson	Johnson State College, John Dewey Library (1955).

Lyndonville	Lyndon State College, Samuel Reed Hall Library (1969).
Middlebury	Middlebury College, Egbert Starr Library (1884).
Montpelier	Vermont State Library (before 1895).
Northfield	Norwich University Library (1908).
Putney	Windham College, Dorothy Culbertson Marvin Memorial Library (1965).

Virgin Islands

Charlotte Amalie (St. Thomas)	St. Thomas Public Library (1968).

Virginia

Blacksburg	Virginia Polytechnic Institute, Newman Library (1907).
Bridgewater	Bridgewater College, Alexander Mack Memorial Library (1902).
Charlottesville	University of Virginia, Alderman Library (1910). REGIONAL
	University of Virginia Law Library (1964).
Chesapeake	Chesapeake Public Library System (1970).
Danville	Danville Community College Library (1969).
Emory	Emory and Henry College Library (1884).
Fairfax	George Mason College of the University of Virginia, Fenwick Library (1960).
Fredericksburg	Mary Washington College of the University of Virginia, E. Lee Trinkel Library (1940).
Hampden-Sydney	Hampden-Sydney College, Eggleston Library (1891).
Hollins College	Hollins College, Fishburn Library (1967).
Lexington	Virginia Military Institute, Preston Library (1874).
	Washington and Lee University, Cyrus Hall McCormick Library (1910).
Norfolk	Armed Forces Staff College Library (1963).
	Norfolk Public Library (1895).
	Old Dominion University, Hughes Memorial Library (1963).
Petersburg	Virginia State College, Johnston Memorial Library (1907).
Quantico	Marine Corps Schools, James Carson Breckinridge Library (1967).

Richmond	University of Richmond, Boatwright Memorial Library (1900).
	Virginia Commonwealth University, James Branch Cabell Library (1971).
	Virginia State Library (unknown).
Roanoke	Roanoke Public Library (1964).
Salem	Roanoke College Library (1886).
Williamsburg	William and Mary College Library (1936).
Wise	Clinch Valley College, John Cook Wyllie Library (1971).

Washington

Bellingham	Western Washington State College, Wilson Library (1963).
Cheney	Eastern Washington State College Library (1966).
Ellensburg	Central Washington State College Library (1962).
Everett	Everett Public Library (1914).
Olympia	Washington State Library (unknown). REGIONAL
Port Angeles	Port Angeles Public Library (1965).
Pullman	Washington State University Library (1907).
Seattle	Seattle Public Library (1908).
	University of Washington Library (1890).
	University of Washington, School of Law Library (1969).
Spokane	Spokane Public Library (1910).
Tacoma	Tacoma Public Library (1894).
	University of Puget Sound, Collins Memorial Library (1938).
Vancouver	Fort Vancouver Regional Library (1962).
Walla Walla	Whitman College, Penrose Memorial Library (1890).

West Virginia

Athens	Concord College Library (1924).
Charleston	Kanawha County Public Library (1952).
	West Virginia Department of Archives and History Library (unknown).
Elkins	Davis and Elkins College Library (1913).
Fairmont	Fairmont State College Library (1884).
Glenville	Glenville State College, Robert F. Kidd Library (1966).
Huntington	Marshall University Library (1925).

Institute	West Virginia State College Library (1907).
Morgantown	West Virginia University Library (1907). REGIONAL
Salem	Salem College Library (1921).
Weirton	Mary H. Weir Public Library (1963).

Wisconsin

Appleton	Lawrence University, Samuel Appleton Library (1869).
Beloit	Beloit College Libraries (1888).
Eau Claire	Wisconsin State University, William D. McIntyre Library (1951).
Fond du Lac	Fond du Lac Public Library (1966).
Green Bay	University of Wisconsin at Green Bay Library (1968).
La Crosse	La Crosse Public Library (1883).
	Wisconsin State University, Murphy Library (1965).
Madison	Department of Public Instruction, Division for Library Services, Reference and Loan Library (1965).
	Madison Public Library (1965).
	State Historical Society Library (1870). REGIONAL
	University of Wisconsin, Memorial Library (1939).
	Wisconsin State Library (unknown).
Milwaukee	Alverno College Library (1971).
	Milwaukee County Law Library (1934).
	Milwaukee Public Library (1861). REGIONAL
	Mount Mary College Library (1964).
	Oklahoma Neighborhood Library (1965).
	University of Wisconsin-Milwaukee Library (1960).
Oshkosh	Wisconsin State University, Forrest R. Polk Library (1956).
Platteville	Wisconsin State University, Elton S. Karrmann Library (1964).
Racine	Racine Public Library (1898).
River Falls	Wisconsin State University, Chalmer Davee Library (1962).
Stevens Point	Wisconsin State University Library (1951).

Superior	Superior Public Library (1908).
	Wisconsin State University, Jim Dan Hill Library (1935).
Waukesha	Waukesha Public Library (1966).
Wausau	Wausau Public Library (1971).
Whitewater	Wisconsin State University, Harold Andersen Library (1963).

Wyoming

Casper	Natrona Country Public Library (1929).
Cheyenne	Wyoming State Library (unknown).
Laramie	University of Wyoming, Coe Library (1907).
Powell	Northwest Community College Library (1967).
Riverton	Central Wyoming College Library (1969).
Rock Springs	Western Wyoming College Library (1969).
Sheridan	Sheridan College, Mary Brown Kooi Library (1963).

1. The libraries listed are designated depositories for Government publications. Information is provided on geographical location, name of the depository library, and the year in which the library became an official depository. The date in which a library assumed official depository status can be useful information for the researcher, for it provides some idea of the chronological scope of the document collection. This list of depositories is updated annually, and the list appears regularly in the September issue of the *Monthly Catalog*. The information in this list is current as of September 1971.

Index